MEARNS MATTERS

a character sketch
of the Glasgow suburb
of Newton Mearns

by
Lesley Williams

Lesley Williams

with illustrations by
Priscilla Dorward

ISBN 0 9512816 0 7

Designed by Heatherbank Press, Milngavie
Printed by Waterside Printers, Blanefield

FOREWORD

Between 1931 and 1951 the population of the Parish of Mearns doubled. It has since doubled again — to twenty thousand or so — as more and more people find the open country environment an attractive place to live and raise a family. Mearns Cross Shopping Centre is built over the old Main Street of the village of 'the Nitton'. Farmlands and the policies of 'the big hooses' have given way to estates of bungalows, blocks of luxury flats, parks, schools, playing fields and golf courses. Agriculture, the traditional way of life for centuries, has almost vanished. Newton Mearns nowadays is a garden-bedecked suburb of the City of Glasgow.

Landmarks of the contemporary scene are set into their past in order to highlight how Mearns matters, and has mattered, to countless folk, both Mearns-born and incoming, throughout this century. Thus through words and images an identity is created for the "new" Newton Mearns.

This book has been compiled with the help of many people to whom Mearns means much. Indeed only through the generous sharing of their experience has the book been possible at all. I thank them all sincerely: this is their book as much as mine. More detailed acknowledgements are made within and after the main text.

Lesley Williams
January 1987

SITUATION, EXTENT and SURFACE

The parish of Mearns is situated in
Renfrewshire. Its centre is about 8
miles distant from Glasgow, and nearly
as far from Paisley. Its length, from
east to west, is 6 miles, and its breadth
about 3½. It stands high above the
level of the Clyde. There are no
considerable hills in it, but the face
of the ground is beautifully diversified
by a great variety of waving swells.
It rises gradually from the east
extremity to the west, where the
moor or commonty lies.

(1st Statistical Account: 1792)

Neilston.

Fingleton Mill

to Stewarton

to Fenwick & Kilmarnock

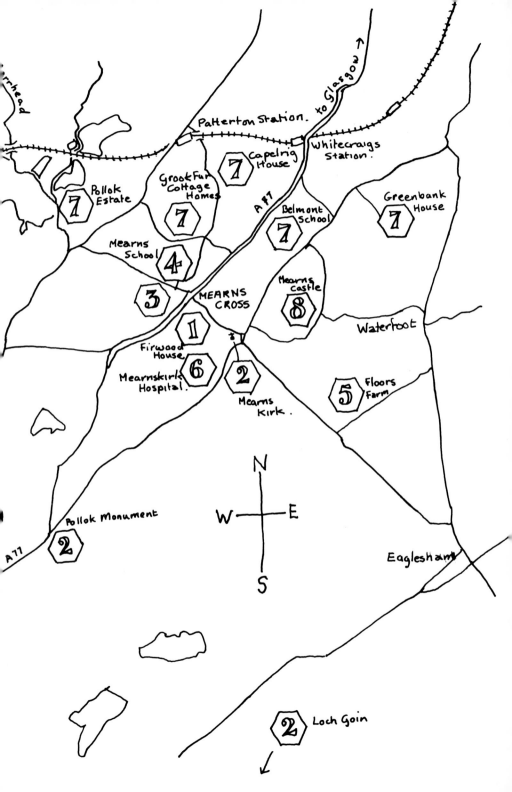

1900......

GARDEN OF EDEN?

I remember sitting in the garden at *Firwood* being read a story about the Garden of Eden and my brother Rob saying, "Yes, that'll just be something like our Mearns."

Thus ninety years on in 1983, Rob's sister Rae Mackinlay recalled her early childhood in Mearns at the turn of the century.

Firwood was built before my time, of course . . . . my father built it to be ready when he married in 1891. After qualifying in medicine and sailing with the Anchor Line to India and to New York, he had settled in Mearns in 1880 . . . . his father had been a doctor in Barrhead and he knew of the vacancy. Probably Barrhead builders built the house, it's so well built . . . . it had a stable and a coach-house and a hay-loft (where we children often hid) . . . . two horses — one would have got tired with all the hills, 'the Poke-hat' especially on the way to Barrhead . . . . Barney was the name of one of them.

From the high garden of our house we looked onto green fields opposite belonging to Townhead Farm . . . . the farm buildings lay behind the stables, garden and yard of the inn at the Cross. This inn faced towards Barrhead and every Friday night we could hear the music from the dance in the inn hall . . . . nobody went but the farm servants, the girls in their striped petticoats and short bodices.

Townhead's fields went as far as Strangs of the Shaw Farm. We used to paddle under the road in the Mearnskirk burn above the Shaw linn. The next dwellings that way were Mr Hunter's school-

house at Mearnskirk and the other wee houses by the church. Across from them was the Red Lion Inn on the hill down to Thumba' Ha'.

Gilmour's fields were at the back of our house, with the farm at Fa'side. Later on an incomer, Fairweather, made it into a 'big hoose' . . . . David Scott the parish minister used to say he'd never learned how long you'd to be in Mearns to become a Mearns man!

I was never a pupil at Mearns School . . . . till I was eleven I went to Miss Osborne's at *Broomlea*, the house next to Mearns School. Three sisters, daughters of the grocer in Barrhead Road, lived there and Miss Margaret used the back parlour as the schoolroom. There were never more than two or three others. I got the three R's, piano and knitting. At eleven I went to the Girls' High in Glasgow for three years . . . . walked to Eastwood Toll and took the red car, Rouken Glen/Riddrie.

We used to go skating on the pond at Hazeldean. The Melvilles who owned Hazeldean bleach and print works did silk printing and sold to Japan . . . . then Japan bought the technology, eventually exports folded and they closed. The works were later demolished. Their son James was at Miss Osborne's school with my brother and me, but he was always plunking and spending the day at the smiddy of Billy Ritchie.

There was a football team, the 'Haddie heids', who always went to Nellie Crine's shop in the Main Street for hot peas and vinegar. Nellie McCabe had a dairy in the front of Burn Cottage (right on the Cross). Mr Wright, the Inspector of Poor, lived in

half of it . . . . tramps who wanted a night's lodging had to report
to him and to my father. Then there was a woman called Mary
Boyle . . . . I remember being terrified just to say "Mary Boyle"
. . . . maybe she was decent enough, but probably would drink.
St Vigean's was the tinkers' lane — they were allowed to camp
there — and at Mearns Castle . . . . I was frightened for them.

My father consulted at home and had a dispensary. He'd an arrangement with the Tofts bleachworks to attend the workers in their 'woman house'. Where a row of thatched cottages stood in the Main Street, my father built a new 'land' for £1,000 and feued the houses. They were called the Doctor's Buildings. I eventually sold them to a Mr Hird for £200—£300 as the rent didn't meet the factoring expenses.

Although the Doctor's Buildings were demolished with the old village Main Street in the 1960s, his name remains in the access road to Mearns School and the Shopping Centre — Mackinlay Place. For older Mearns folk, of course, the name Mackinlay triggers off a series of affectionate memories, among them the following from Mr Craig, who grew up on Wellmeadow Farm:

7

The doctor was a conspicuous figure with striped trousers, a cream flowered waistcoat, double-breasted. In one of his pockets he kept a thermometer. He never carried a bag, although Nurse Deas did, but kept all the tools of his profession in one of the tails of his morning coat. He bought an Arrol Johnston motor car when cars started to take the place of horses and he and Nurse Deas could be seen driving along about 5 mph, he never changed gear from first. He was never too fond of that mode of travel and more often walked with Nurse Deas to visit patients. If we saw them on our way to school we'd say to each other,

"There's the Doctor and the Nurse, stand and salute." Which one and all did.

He pulled teeth in the Laundry part of *Firwood* with the patient sitting in an old basket chair, as dentists were not even heard of in Mearns . . . . no cocaine or other jags . . . . just a strong arm round the neck where the hand could get the patient's jaw . . . . then in went the forceps and after a struggle the patient invariably managed to get to his feet and the two did a waltz about the Laundry . . . . the tooth was out . . . . the Doctor stood triumphant with the tooth in the forceps, while the patient was down the back drive, holding his jaw, hearing the Doctor call, "It's out. I have it here."

In Eaglesham Road Dr Mackinlay's family home *The Firs* or *Firwood* continues to command an extensive view; nowadays, however, of gardens and rooftops rather than open fields and farms. And still from Mearns Cross, past *Firwood* eastwards, the road winds up and down to the Puddock Ford, up and down to the bridge the young Mackinlays paddled under in the Mearnskirk burn, and up to Mearns Kirk, the crowning landmark of what was once a country parish of farms, moorland, village, and the occasional country house.

Old Mearns Church from Eaglesham Road

MOST GLADSOME PARISH
kirk, cattle, countryside and Covenanters

The original centre of the parish was not as one might have expected at Mearns Cross, but at Mearnskirk. There inn, school, rows of cottages and smiddy clustered along the ridge crowned by the Kirk of the Parish. The present church building dates from 1813. Legend, however, associates a Celtic church of St Bride with the site. Records show that in the Middle Ages money was sent to Paisley Abbey; indeed rumour has it that *all* the Kirk money went to Paisley in return for the monks there saying prayers for the souls of the Mearns dead. Thus, the Kirk at Mearns was perpetually impoverished. Be that as it may, congregations have worshipped here since pre-Reformation times.

*Junction of Eaglesham Road with Old Mearns Road
(now Kirkview Crescent)*

Stones in the graveyard date from 1742. One of the best preserved is the horizontal stone commemorating the ministry of the Rev Dr McLatchie:

IN MEMORY OF
THE
REV GEORGE McLATCHIE D.D.
late Minister
of the Parish of Mearns

He was ordained Assistant
and successor to the

REV ALEXANDER CRUIKSHANK
in this Parish
on the 11th April 1786

Succeeded him on his death
on 22nd January 1791

And died on the 13th August
1833
Aged 76 years

He was beloved as a Pastor
and regretted by all who knew him.

— — — — — — — — —

This is erected by his friend
NEIL C. HUTCHISON
Anno 1836

In March 1824 Dr McLatchie was
succeeded by the REV DONALD MACKELLAR
who continued Minister of this Parish
till his death on 6th January 1868

To Dr McLatchie, an incomer two hundred years ago, fell the duty of contributing with all the other parish ministers in Scotland to the *First Statistical Account*. This is the earliest

13

extended writing which describes our district. Under the editorship of Sir John Sinclair, between 1791 and 1798 twenty-one volumes describing every shire in Scotland were published: subtitled "an enquiry into the country for the purpose of ascertaining the quantum of happiness enjoyed by its inhabitants and the means of its future improvement." Surveys and reports are not new!

Dr McLatchie had a high regard for his parishioners, describing them thus:

> The people of this parish are sober, industrious, and economical; respectful to their superiors and uncommonly friendly and obliging.
>
> They are rational in their religious sentiments and moderate in their religious zeal. All of them are strongly attached to our present civil constitution and cautiously avoid giving countenance to any change or innovation in it. It is happy for them that they pretend not to make politics their study. They mind the duties and business of their own station, and wish to enjoy with thankfulness and peace the many blessings which a kind providence bestows on them.

Born in 1757, Dr McLatchie was 19 when the American colonists declared their independence from the Britain of King George III; and 32 when the Fall of the Bastille heralded the French Revolution. He came to Mearns in 1786 and may well have been writing his account of the parish when King Louis XVI and his Queen Marie Antoinette were executed in 1792 with many of the French aristocracy. He was pleased, therefore, to observe no radical tendencies among his flock. Mearns has perhaps a long history of conservatism!

Fifty years later a further survey was published – the *Second* or *New Statistical Account*, to which Dr McLatchie's successor, Mr MacKellar contributed the information about the Parish of Mearns. He too was pleased with the character of the inhabitants.

> As this is strictly a rural district, the people are characterised to a certain extent by simplicity of manners and by an absence of many of the vices that are more common and more fashionable in populous manufacturing districts.

Both ministers help us to picture the rural Mearns of earlier days. Dairying predominated.

> The soil is all of a light and quick kind . . . . chiefly remarkable for its fine pasture. It produces grass both in greater quantity than common and likewise of the very best kind, and it everywhere abounds with a profusion of white clover. The greater part of the land is in pasturage.
>
> Every farm is stocked with milk cows; and the principal object of the farmer is to produce butter and butter-milk for the Glasgow market. The butter that is made here, and especially that which is salted for winter use, is reckoned preferable to any other and the demand for it is vastly greater than can be answered. It has nothing of that rancid taste which butter made on deeper and heavier soils is sometimes found to have; and it keeps in good condition for a very long time.
>
> The dairy cows are all of the Ayrshire breed, are finely formed, and of the best stock. Butter and butter-milk are here manufactured in a style not surpassed in any other district in the west of Scotland. The Mearns butter is farmed in Glasgow and Paisley and families are anxious to lay in their winter butter, the veritable produce of the celebrated dairies of the Mearns.

15

The churning of milk makes a great and laborious part of the farmers' work. Of late they have introduced the use of churning-mills driven by water. There are many streams that run through the parish and answer for these mills, and on trial they prove highly beneficial and save a great deal of labour.

DUNCARNOCK AND GLANDERSTON DAM, NEWTON MEARNS

Not surprisingly one of the social highlights of the rural Mearns calendar was the annual Cattle Show, run by Mearns Agricultural Society on the last Saturday of April "at 11 o'clock prompt." The 1919 Show had 24 classes for Ayrshire Cattle, 14 for Milk Stock and 10 for Bulls & Yeld Stock; 14 classes for Clydesdale Horses and a further 7 Horse classes; 6 sheep classes for Leicesters, Blackfaced, and Crossbreeds; 14 Poultry classes; best Collie Dog or Bitch; best Oatcakes, Soda Scones, Potato Scones, Pancakes, Shortbread, and Jelly Sponge. Cash prizes were usually awarded, but depending on the allocation of the many donations in kind, other prizes might be won. A felt hat (valued at a guinea), donated by Kirsops, was won by the competitor showing the best

16

Leicester. In the Ayrshire Milk Stock classes the highest First Prizes were £2 and up to five awards might be made in any one class.

The rationale underlying the allocation of the prizes is lost in history. Here are some examples chosen from the Ayrshire Cattle classes:

1.   COW IN MILK, calved before 1st Jan 1916

First			£2	0 0
Second			1	0 0
Third				17 6
Fourth	Purse	value		10 0
Fifth	Pail	value		7 6

2.   BEST COW or QUEY in CALF or MILK Bred in the Parish

First			1	10 0
Second			1	0 0
Third	Box Toilet Soap	value		14 0
Fourth				5 0

3.   THREE YEAR OLD COW IN MILK

First			1 0 0
Second			10 0
Third	Pair of Slippers	value	7 6

10.   BACK CALVING COW, FOUR YEARS OLD & UPWARDS
not to calve before 1st Aug. or later than 1st Jan. 1920

First	Bag of Feeding Meal	value	2 0 0
Second			1 0 0
Third			10 0
Fourth			5 0

11.   PAIR OF BACK CALVING COWS, not to calve before
1st August or later than 1st Jan. 1920

First	Roast of Beef	value	1 0 0
Second			15 0
Third			10 0

13.   BEST COW IN CALF or MILK, with an official Milk
      Record (as a cow or quey) of over 800 gallons
      First   2   0 0
      Second   1 10 0
      Third   1   0 0
      Fourth   10 0

Competitors in Class 13 were also eligible for a Special Prize presented by the Lanarkshire and Renfrewshire Hunt.

Milking Competitions ran for SENIORS — any age — and JUNIORS — 14 years and under — for the "Quickest and Best Milker. Competitors provide own Cow which must give at least 12lbs of milk at Milking."

Entries were booked with the Show Secretary at Newton Inn "between Six and Eight o'clock" on the previous evening. Any Animal gaining a First Prize in the same class for two years was not allowed to compete in that Class again. All protests had to be lodged in writing with the Secretary on the day of the Show, along with a deposit of 20s which was returned if the protest was sustained. Prize money was paid at the General Meeting of Members in August and any unclaimed by 1st October sent to the winner less 5%.

The day's programme ran:

9	Show Yard opens
9 to 10.45	Placing of Stock
10.45	Judges, Stewards, etc. meet in Secretary's Tent
11	Judging Commences
12.30	Milking Competition
1 to 2.15	Luncheon
2.15	Judging Horses Commences
4.30	Jumping Competition

MUSIC WILL BE DISCOURSED DURING THE AFTERNOON

18

"Luncheon" was the focus of the day for all self-respecting and proper participants. A full page notice in the Prize List reminded members of their social obligations:

THE DINNER
will be held in
THE UNIONIST ROOMS
BARRHEAD ROAD, about 1 p.m.
CHARGE 5/-

– – – – – –

Train from Central Station, Glasgow, to Giffnock and Whitecraigs. Motor Buses to and from Mearns will run at intervals between the Car terminus and Giffnock and Whitecraigs Railway Stations, during the day.

Competitors gaining more than 10/- Prize Money will require to dine or forfeit 5/-; this penalty will be enforced.

Alex. Garvie, Hon. Secretary.
Plenploth, Newton Mearns, April, 1919.

Those who could not afford or did not qualify for the official luncheon bought pies at Hay's the baker in Barrhead Road. Demand was such that

the week before the Show my father had to employ an extra baker from Glasgow – he lodged for the week in Ashview Terrace – and from about 4 o'clock every morning right through the day we made hundreds and hundreds of twopenny pies (meat from Johnson's) and tarts – all the farmer people bought them – to eat them and to take away: "I'll just pick up a couple of dozen on the way home from the Show", they'd say.

The Show itself was held "on Mr Gilmour's Field adjoining Newton Mearns", an easy walk from the Unionist Rooms. Three

19

Barrhead Road, Newton Mearns

hundred and eighty-seven separately itemised donations funded the 1919 Show. Most donors gave 5/-, 10/- or one guinea, in return for which they could compete in the Show and read their name on the Donor List. The 387 names were grouped by amount alphabetically within each category. Donations ranged from the 5 guineas of Sir Thomas Clement of Barcaple to "under 5/- from A Soldier"; Mrs Mather of Kirkhill House and Mr Hannay of The Broom each gave £1, more or less the going 'big house' rate; Dr Mackinlay gave 10/- as did one of Mearns's grocers, the other settling for 5/-; and in between at 7/6 was the donation of Mr Downie, the Headmaster. All in all 387 patrons contributed £204.11/6. That year 21 gifts were received, some of which have been already mentioned as prizes in the Ayrshire classes. Others included a silver fern pot, a steel graip, a £6 chest of finest tea, two whips and an umbrella. Admission charges increased the revenue – 1s for adults and 6d for juveniles – a lot of money in these days. Enterprising juveniles of course found other ways in. Village families all enjoyed the spectacle of the fully dressed

Clydesdales as they passed along Main Street on their way to the Show field.

What a great day the Cattle Show was . . . . in the morning the clip clop of the big horses – the Clydesdales – their tails all tied up– along the Main Street . . . . the houses were all cleaned and whitewashed for the Cattle Show . . . . then the cows . . . . and the hens . . . . everyone came in from all around for the Shows at night–Christmas was nothing compared to it.

Agriculture in Mearns had reached a very sopisticated level in the hundred years since Dr McLatchie and Mr MacKellar were praising its butter production. And greater changes were not far away. Let's return, however, to the days of Dr McLatchie to savour a little more of a way of life soon to vanish in face of the growth of Glasgow, a way of life now wholly gone from Mearns.

Poor – There are but few poor in the parish. These are supported in the usual way; by collections made at the church, by the interest of a small accumulated fund, by the profits of the mort-cloth, and by dues arising from the publication of the banns of marriage. There are no begging poor belonging to the parish.

School – There is a parochial schoolmaster who has a salary of £8.6s.8d sterling besides the usual small school fees and an allowance of 30s as Session Clerk. There is the same reason to complain here, as in most other places, that the emoluments of the schoolmaster are in no way adequate to the qualifications expected and to the labour and fatigue required.

Church – Sir Michael Stewart of Blackhall, Bart. is patron. The stipend is 5 chalders of meal, and £27.13s sterling of money. No augmentation has ever yet been demanded. The glebe consists of about 4 acres of arable land. A very good manse was built in 1789 and the church was fitted up in a very neat and commodious manner in 1792.

There has long been an Anti-burgher meeting-house here. The congregation, which is not near so numerous now as formerly, is made up of people belonging to this parish and to some of the adjoining parishes.

There are likewise in the parish a few Burghers and Cameronians. It is pleasant to see the happy effects of toleration. Time has softened the rancour of party among these seceders from the Established Church, and almost all of them live in good neighbourhood and discover a spirit of Christian charity and moderation.

To Dr McLatchie's "very good manse" – doubtless a happy supplement to his stipend of "5 chalders of meal and £27.13s sterling of money" – came young men to prepare for entrance to university.

Among his boarders from 1807 to 1811 was a Paisley boy, John Wilson, who later became Professor of Moral Philosophy at Edinburgh University. Those were the days when Edinburgh was styled The Athens of the North. Under the nom-de-plume of Christopher North, Professor Wilson became famous throughout Britain through the satirical articles he contributed to *Blackwoods Magazine.*

Mr Wilson, Senior, a Paisley merchant, had chosen to send his son to Dr McLatchie's manse to ensure a sound classical education in the healthy moorland environment of the Mearns. John Wilson later nostalgically recalled his boyhood haunts in a collection of autobiographical essays called "Recreations of Christopher North", especially in the essays entitled 'Our Parish' and 'May-Day' (1842).

Our boyhood was environed by the Beautiful –
　　　　　　its home was among moors . . . .
the cheerfullest and most gladsome parish
　　　　　　in all braid Scotland . . . .
as for its name, men call it Mearns.

Art thou beautiful, as of old,
Oh wild moorland, sylvan and pastoral parish? . . . .

Fairest of Scotland's thousand parishes —
neither highland or lowland —
but undulating like the sea in the sunset
after a day of storms . . . .

Thou art indeed beautiful as of old!

Fishing was a frequent pastime with the young scholars, their favourite burn being —

the Yearn — endearingly called the Humby, from a farm near the manse and belonging to the minister.

The best beloved, if not the most beautiful, of all the lochs was the Brother Loch . . . . tradition assigned the name on account of three brothers that perished in its waters . . . . above all, it was the loch for angling.

Christopher North glowingly portrayed a highlight of the local social calendar —

The Brother Loch saw annually another sight, when on Green Brae was pitched a tent — a snow-white pyramid gathering to itself all the sunshine.

There lords and ladies and knights and squires celebrated old May-Day and half the parish flocked to the festival.

The Earl of Eglintoun, and Sir Michael Shaw-Stewart and old Sir John of Polloc, and Pollock of that Ilk, and other heads of illustrious houses — with their wives and daughters, a beautiful show — did not disdain them of low degree but kept open table on the moor;
and
would you believe it
high born youths and maidens ministered at the board to cottage lads and lasses, whose sunburned faces hardly dared to smile under awe of that courtesy — yet whenever they looked up there was happiness in their eyes.

The young ladies were all arrayed in green; and after the feast they took bows and arrows in their lily hands and shot at a target in a style that would have gladdened the heart of Maid Marion — nay of Robin himself.

A more everyday group for the young scholars to encounter was —

> a party of divot-flaughterers . . . . the people of the parish are now digging their peats . . . . here is a whole household, provident for winter, borrowing fuel from the moss.

Lunch-time rest might include "a strathspey frae the fiddle o' auld blin' Hugh Lyndsay, the itinerant musicianer" and a game of "loup-the-barrows" in which the young scholars from the manse strove to outjump the local boys. Dr McLatchie's young scholars clearly had plenty of freedom from their studies and, like all who have had the good fortune to grow up in Mearns, found it a good place to be.

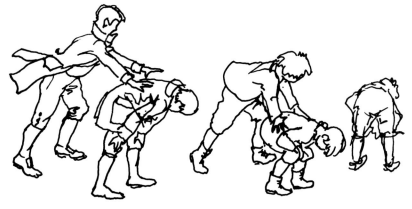

Mearns Parish Kirk enjoys a commanding site and is widely visible throughout the parish it serves. The gateposts at the entry to the kirkyard are hollow with room inside for a sentry. In the days when there was reputed to be a market with anatomists for cadavers, relatives of the recently deceased, armed with cudgels, or even blunderbusses, stood there to protect the newly buried body. Perhaps West of Scotland admirers of Burke and Hare made body-snatching raids on Mearns kirkyard. The Anatomy Act of 1832 ended such worries.

On a cheerier note, in the earlier years of the present century hot pies and glasses of porter were served at the *Red Lion Inn* to parishioners who walked or rode to morning worship from a distance and who often stayed over the "interval" for a further service in the afternoon. Horses could be stabled in the Inn yard. A pail of water and a drinking cup stood by the church gateway — beside the collection plate — to refresh those dry from their walk up to the kirk.

the old Red Lion
a Coaching Inn

There's a story behind the weather cock. The present phosphor bronze bird weighs 2½ cwts and was set atop the steeple shortly after the War. It replaced an earlier "bird" which had lost part of its tail years before when two shooting patrons from the *Red Lion* hit their target. While a prisoner of war the Rev. Drummond Duff (minister from 1929–51) was promised by a fellow prisoner from Hazeldean that if they both survived the War, as a thank-offering he would present the church with a new weathercock.

25

Dr McLatchie commented that the church was "fitted up in a very neat and commodious manner." He would find equal pleasure in its "fittings" today. In 1931 and 1932 the interior was wholly renovated and the present chancel built out from the north wall. The plain glass windows on the south wall were replaced by stained glass, one depicting the disciple Andrew and the other Queen Margaret, patron saint of the church in Scotland. Many lovely windows have been added since. The present organ is the result of an appeal launched in 1982 to celebrate the jubilee of the renovation.

Following the Second World War, within the four acre glebe a modern manse and new halls have been built. The old manse, diagonally opposite at the corner of Humbie Road, is now divided into flats and three smaller houses share its grounds. Present day ministers would not have room to board boys studying for university as Dr McLatchie did. Nor the domestic staff! Once the new halls were ready, the old hall (on Ayr Road opposite Mearns School) was sold to the Jewish community.

Dr McLatchie recognised that even in his days of fairly universal church-going, not all the people of the parish attended his church. He alluded to an Anti-burgher meeting house and other seceding groups, remarking that time had softened "the rancour of party among these seceders from the Established Church" and "almost all of them live in good neighbourhood and discover a spirit of Christian charity and moderation."

Newton Mearns Parish Church of Scotland and Maple Evangelical Church, both at Mearns Cross, trace their origins to this Seceder tradition. During the eighteenth century the Anti-burgher meeting houses or churches in Main Street drew their congregations from as far off as Neilston and Eaglesham. 1839 saw the opening of a church large enough to seat four hundred and which became part of the United Presbyterian Church from 1847; subsequently the United Free Church of Scotland, which in turn united with the Church of Scotland in 1929. Among the Communion plate is a pewter paten stamped with a ship in full sail squarely bordered with the words "Success to the United States of America", reminding us that many of those who dissented from the practices of the established churches in Scotland and England chose to cross the Atlantic

to seek freedom of worship. When the custom of a Precentor leading the praise gave 'way to the use of an organ, it is said that a Malletsheugh worthy who had attended church every Sunday of his long life promptly stopped coming, declaring that the organ was a "kist of whustles".

The longest Mearns ministry of this century is that of the Rev. W. Murray Mackay who served Newton Mearns Parish Church from 1931 to 1976. As a young minister one of his first tasks was to oversee the building of the present church at Mearns Cross. On 10th December 1938 Mrs Templeton of Crookfur laid the Memorial Stone and a year later the Dedication Service was conducted. Stones from the previous church were used in the internal walls, and in the vestibule stones dated 1743 and 1754

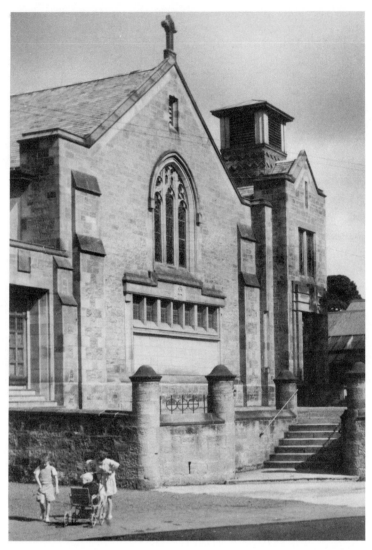

come from the earlier church buildings. The post-war photograph shows the addition of a bell-tower, one of the gifts of the Young family in memory of their son Robert who was killed in the Second World War. The sheds of Johnson's Ironmongery business have gone – replaced by the Library, the Trustee Savings Bank and the second hall of Newton Mearns Church.

A long ministry like Mr Mackay's has been by no means unique in the annals of the Newton Mearns congregation. The first two ministers — Andrew Thomson, father and son — served from 1746 until 1816. Originally a Praying Society, the congregation itself dates from 1738 and built its first church in 1743. One of the children baptised in 1798 by Andrew the son was Robert Pollok. A century ago the fame of this young poet, who died in 1827 in his 29th year, was quite remarkable. Now he is unknown, even within his own parish. His fame rested on an epic poem "The Course of Time" running to three hundred pages. Published in Edinburgh in 1827 it won great critical acclaim, one London reviewer even ranking Pollok "in the good company of Dante and Milton". Within forty years of his death over 78,000 copies had been sold.

Among Robert Pollok's earlier writings were stories about the Covenanters, set on the moors where he was raised. From Moorhouse Farm (south of Eastwood Golf Course) he walked for six years to Mearns Parish School, then at Mearnskirk. The schooling there was described favourably by Mr MacKellar in his 1842 contribution to the *Second Statistical Account:*

Education — The parish school-room is one of the largest and airiest of any in the west of Scotland. Mr Jackson, the very able and excellent teacher, has long laboured with much success in his very important and useful sphere as parochial teacher. According to the last official returns, the number of children attending the parish school was 103, attending other schools, 150. The branches taught in the parish school are Latin, geography, arithmetic, English grammar, reading and writing. The salary of the parochial teacher is £34.4s., school-fees £63, with £4 annually from other sources. There is a school at Busby and a small country school besides. There are few, if any, natives above fifteen years of age who cannot read the Scriptures, and who have not been taught to write.

From Mr Jackson's tutelage Robert and his elder brother David transferred to Fenwick where Mr John Fairlie advanced their Latin studies in preparation for entry to Glasgow University. During the school week the boys boarded with an uncle and, according to David in his "Life of Robert Pollok", it was while walking the eight miles between Moorhouse and Horsehill,

Fenwick, that Robert began composing poetry in his head. Next to the Bible, Milton was his favourite author, hardly a surprising preference for a young man brought up in the Seceder/ Covenanting tradition.

Like his mentor Milton, Robert Pollok did not at first aspire to be a full-time writer. His university studies were directed towards the ministry and he became licensed as a preacher of the United Secession Church. Ill-health prevented his seeking a charge. Following the publication of "The Course of Time" well-wishers contributed to his wintering in Italy, whither he sailed from Leith with his sister in September 1827. He died en route. In the Southampton graveyard where he was buried, the headstone reads simply:

> The Grave of Robert Pollok, A.M.,
> Author of "The Course of Time".
> His Immortal Poem is his Monument
>   Erected by Admirers of his Genius.

Early verses celebrate his moorland home "far from the madding crowd".

> Time-worn Moorhouse . . . .
>   placed far remote
> From city broils and treason's plot:
> Far from the crimes that rage unnamed,
> From which the day retires ashamed.
>   . . . .
> Thy walls a faithful shelter proved
> To those that food and virtue loved.
> Within thy walls assembled saints
> Praised Him who wearies not nor faints.
>
>   . . . .

31

Happy swains who in thee live,
Who read their Bibles and believe,
Who worship God with heart and mind,
And to His will are aye resigned!

NORTH MOORHOUSE
Pollok's Birthplace

Throughout the nineteenth century Pollok's work was held in high esteem and his birthplace at Moorhouse was on the itinerary of many a walker from Glasgow. One such was Hugh Macdonald of 62 John Street, Bridgeton. In 1854 as 'Caleb' of the *Glasgow Citizen* he published 21 "Rambles Round Glasgow, with a resume of the Historical, Biographical and Traditional associations of the various localities". In *Walk No. IX* he joined Robert Pollok's brother David for a walk from Waterfoot up the River Earn to the Moorhouses and beyond.

Let's join them as they savour the fresh moorland air of the upland parishes of Eaglesham and Mearns:

Passing Humbie Brig and the fine farm of Titwood, we soon arrive at the bleach works of Hazelden, where we cross to the south or Eaglesham side of the Earn. A few minutes' walk further, during which we passed Hazelden Head, Hazelden Mains, and various other places with Hazelden prefixes, brings us to the lands of North Moorhouse, the birthplace of Robert Pollok, the gifted author of *The Course of Time*.

The banks of the stream are here of the most beautiful description. On either side they rise in softest verdure, to a con-

32

siderable height in natural terraces, some of which are scooped out into smooth green dells. This indentation looks as if it had been designed for a Covenanting place of worship.

We encounter two votaries of the 'gentle art', earnestly lashing the rippled bosom of the stream.

"Well, what luck have ye had today, lads?"

"Oh, jist middlin'" was the reply of the foremost disciple of Izaak, "the water's ower clear an' the licht ower strang the day for burn-trout."

"We've had a rise or two, though," interposed the other, "and I daursay, if we had two-three worms, we micht dae no that ill yet."

Patience and hope are indeed necessary mental qualifications for successful angling.

Immediately after taking leave of the anglers, we pass a little ford where the Moorhouse people are in the habit of crossing the stream when making a 'short cut' to the village of Mearns. Many a time and oft the future poet had 'buckled his breeks' and forded the Earn at this spot when on his way to school at the Kirktoun.

Seventy years later in the heyday of tram cars, the Corporation of Glasgow Transport Department featured the Moorhouse area in their official guide to the "Romantic and Beautiful Countryside Around the City". T.C.F. Brotchie was the author and artist of this 1920 guide. He walked the five or six miles from the tram terminus at Clarkston Toll (fare from Jamaica Street 3d) and sketched North Moorhouse farm where Pollok had been born. The lines from Pollok's verse which Brotchie quoted describe trees at Mid Moorhouse where the poet lived from his seventh year.

> Tall trees they were
> And old and had been old a century
> Before my day. None living could say aught
> About their youth; but they were goodly trees,
> And oft I wondered as I sat and thought
> Beneath their summer shade, or in the night
> Of winter heard the spirits of the wind
> Growling among their boughs, how they had grown
> So high in such a rough tempestuous place.

33

COVENANTING COUNTRY

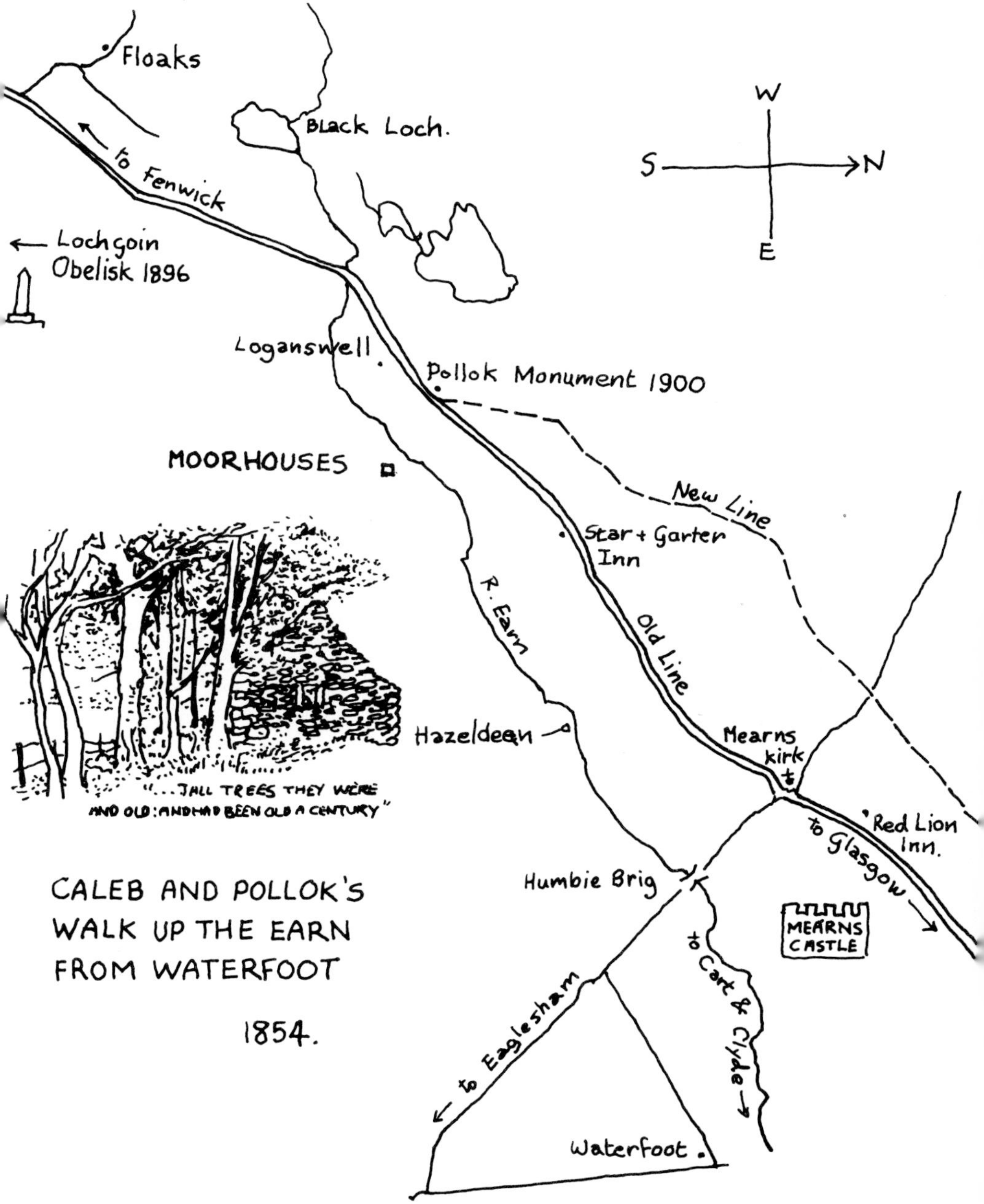

• Floaks

Black Loch.

W
S ———+——→ N
E

to Fenwick

← Lochgoin
Obelisk 1896

Loganswell •

Pollok Monument 1900

MOORHOUSES ▫

New Line

• Star + Garter
Inn

R. Earn

Old Line

"...TALL TREES THEY WERE
AND OLD: AND HAD BEEN OLD A CENTURY"

Hazeldean ⟋

Mearns
kirk
✝

• Red Lion
Inn.

to Glasgow →

CALEB AND POLLOK'S
WALK UP THE EARN
FROM WATERFOOT

1854.

Humbie Brig

MEARNS
CASTLE

← to Eaglesham

to Cart & Clyde →

Waterfoot •

Only two of Pollok's "tall trees" remained in that "rough tempestuous place". Brotchie saw a

> windswept solitary spot, 830 feet above sea level and exposed to every wind that blows — a forgotten, neglected spot . . . . now little more than a gable end.

A monument to the poet, commissioned to celebrate the centenary of his birth, was unveiled on 24th September 1900. It stands at Logans Well at the junction of the A77 and the Mearns-kirk road. In his speech of dedication the Rev. James Mather of the United Presbyterian Church, Dalry, Galloway, concluded:

> Stand there! thou sky-aspiring granite, taken from the heart of Galloway, a thing of beauty and of silent might, happily wed to the name of one in whom strength found his castle and beauty her palace.

The granite stone with its bronze medallion bears this eloquent
tribute to Robert Pollok: "He soared untrodden heights and
seemed at home."

Caleb in the 1850s and Brotchie in the 1920s are representative
of the many walkers who sought a change from the smoky industrial city of Glasgow to the fresh moorland air of upland
Mearns. For their further refreshment a new institution was
created — the tearoom. At Mearns Cross, *The Neuk* and *The
Bungalow*, at Loganswell *The Red House*, two more at Hazeldene,

one each at Pilmuir, Malletsheugh and Patterton. Near-by farms found a new market for their eggs with parties of ramblers booking in for ham and egg teas on Saturday evenings. Travellers previously had depended upon the old coaching inns – *Red Lion, Star and Garter, Turf, Kingswell, Newton,* and *Malletsheugh.* Only

old Malletsheugh Inn

the *Malletsheugh*, albeit in an entirely new building, remains.

Until 1832 the south/north routes through the district followed the line of the present Stewarton Road to Spiersbridge or ran from Fenwick via the Floaks, Loganswell, and Mearnskirk to Clarkston. This latter route became known as the 'Old Line' after the construction of a 'New Line' (the present A77) from Loganswell via Mearns Cross to Giffnock. This new road with its macadamised surface, the technique pioneered by John Macadam in Ayrshire at the turn of the nineteenth century, contributed to the shift in the centre of parish life from Mearnskirk to the village of the Newton. The *Star and Garter Inn* on the 'Old Line' between

THE STAR
AND
GARTER INN

Loganswell and Mearnskirk closed and became a farm. It is now a private house. Improved road surfaces along with the later inventions of the bicycle, the pneumatic tyre, and the internal combustion engine gradually led to swifter communication between Mearns and Glasgow. This radically changed our area. From a rural parish of scattered farmtouns and a two-street village where people lived and worked, Mearns has changed to a suburb, most of whose residents commute to work in Glasgow.

Nellies Toll Gi, Mearns Rd.

Originally the 'New Line' was maintained by tolls collected a the Floaks, Loganswell, and Eastwood Toll. Rates varied according to load. A vehicle drawn by six horses was charged 4/- Scots (4d English), the levy being reduced if fewer horses were used. Cattle passed the toll at 10d per score. Sledges (which may have been used in muddy conditions as well as in icy or snowy weather) cost 4½d. Carts carrying materials for building and paving Glasgow streets paid no tolls. Many loads of lime, coal, grain, wood, and other supplies were packed into panniers and slung across the backs of ponies. Glasgow markets were about a two hour ride. A horse, laden or otherwise, if not drawing a vehicle paid 3d toll. All tolls were abolished in 1865.

Eastwood tollhouse, after a spell as Nellie Niven's sweetie shop, was demolished in 1907. Loganswell lasted till the mid-century. Beyond the Loganswell tollhouse, with its little shop at the front, was Loganswell School — until 1928 when the sole teacher, Mrs Bell, and seven pupils were transferred to Mearns. An anecdote from a Loganswell former pupil highlights the quietness of even the main roads in these early days of the century:

> Mrs Stewart was absent once — during the Spanish flu' epidemic at the end of the War, I think it was — and Miss Maver came up daily from Mearns School . . . . she came by cab driven by Johnny Cannon in his tile hat. One time we hurled the blackboard out into the middle of the road and Minnie Ross was playing at being teacher — she was the wildest girl that ever was — I was the 'watcher' for Johnny Cannon's hat coming round the corner . . . .

The speed of the approaching cab easily permitted a successful withdrawal of the blackboard before Miss Maver made her entry.

The pace of life in these early days of the twentieth century had changed little in hundreds of years. In his idealised portrayal of the Mearns of his boyhood, Christopher North re-created a scene of travellers relaxing at the 'Salutation Inn' and marvelling at the capacity and speed of

The Highflier Coach! carrying six in and twelve outside — driver and guard excluded — rate of motion eleven miles per hour, with stoppages. Why, in the name of Heaven, are all people nowadays in such haste and hurry?

Confident are we that the obese elderly gentleman beside the coachman needed not to have been so carried in a whirlwind to his comfortable home. Scarcely is there time for pity as we behold an honest man's wife, pale as putty in the face, at a tremendous swing, a lunge, or lurch of the Highflier, holding on like grim death to the balustrades.

But umbrellas, parasols, plaids, shawls, bonnets and greatcoats with as many necks as Hydra — the Pile of Life has disappeared in a cloud of dust, and the faint bugle tells that already it has spun and reeled onwards a mile on its destination.

Prior to today's heavy volume of fast-flowing traffic, the highways and byways around Mearns were a pleasure to walk and cycle. Returning to Caleb as an example, from Moorhouse he continued his walk southwards and upwards to where the River Earn is formed by the confluence of the burns from the Floaks with the burn from Black Loch.

We are now at the head of the vale and in the very heart of the Mearns Moor.

Around us on every side a dreary expanse of brown heathy hills and dark morasses stretches away to the horizon. Here and there a few comparatively fertile spots enliven the waste; each with a cluster of ash trees and a little wreath of blue smoke marking the sites of the thin strewn pastoral farms.

Yet there is a peculiar beauty in the wild landscape, all black and dreary as it is . . . . the peesweep flutters round our head and the snipe starts from our path on its tortuous flight, while at our feet we have the meeting of the waters which form the lovely Earn . . . . there is a pleasing harmony in the music of their many waters.

The age of kelpies is past, we fear, but were it not so, we should almost expect to find one of these water-demons lurking among the plashy nooks below our present position.

41

The moors were not always as still and desolate as Caleb found them. In common with north Ayrshire and western Lanarkshire, the moorlands of east Renfrewshire are steeped in legends and history of the Covenanters. The moorland triangle bounded by Mearns, Eaglesham and Fenwick is Covenanting heartland. Conventicles with hundreds of worshippers were held in the hollows of the moors. Even yet, if walking or golfing at East Renfrewshire, Eastwood, or Bonnyton, it is not difficult to imagine sentries posted on knolls and ridges to alert the worshippers to any sign of Government soldiers. At the Floaks on the Mearns/Fenwick boundary the Covenanting captain John Paton was captured and in May 1684 hanged in the Grassmarket in Edinburgh. In these stirring days of the Covenant many a family sacrificed property, and even life, for their faith.

As an impecunious student, lodged in a Crown Street tenement, while at Glasgow University, to help make ends meet Robert Pollok published his first writings, three tales of the Covenanters: "The Persecuted Family", "Ralph Gemmill" and "Ellen of the Glen". One of his source books would definitely have been John Howie's biography "The Scots Worthies", which from its appearance in 1775 became a standard classic on the subject of the Scottish Covenant. John Howie farmed at Lochgoin where

Lochgoin and Fenwick Covenanters Trust
Lochgoin Farmhouse - 1969

conventicles were so frequent in his great-grandparents' days that
it was raided twelve times. A tall granite obelisk commemorating
John Howie and the famous men whose lives he recounted has
stood since 1896 on the 'Top' near Lochgoin Farm at the point
where Covenanting guards kept a lookout for the troopers. On
their warning, the household and any fugitives would flee to the
safety of the bogs and morasses which stretched for miles behind
the farmhouse. Inscribed on the monument is a verse from Psalm
77, "I have considered the days of old", a fitting tribute to John
Howie. The 'worthies' named on the plinth are

KNOX   HENDERSON   RENWICK   CARGILL   CAMERON
MELVILLE   PEDEN   ARGYLE   RUTHERFORD
JOHN BROWN   BLACKADDER   McPHAIL   LOUDOUN
PATON   NISBET   GILLESPIE   GUTHRIE

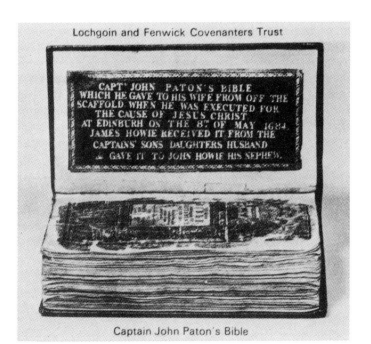

CAPT. JOHN PATON'S BIBLE WHICH HE GAVE TO HIS WIFE FROM OFF THE SCAFFOLD WHEN HE WAS EXECUTED FOR THE CAUSE OF JESUS CHRIST AT EDINBURH ON THE 8TH OF MAY 1684. JAMES HOWIE RECEIVED IT FROM THE CAPTAINS' SONS DAUGHTERS HUSBAND & GAVE IT TO JOHN HOWIE HIS NEPHEW.

Captain John Paton's Bible

At a conventicle on 23rd July 1967, convened in the shadow of the monument, the late Lord Rowallan gifted Lochgoin Farm to the *Fenwick and Lochgoin Covenanters' Trust.* Within the farm-house a small museum is maintained, which is open to the public and easily reached by car. The single track access road is clearly signed off the Kilmarnock/Eaglesham road about a mile north of its junction with the A77. Among the exhibits are Captain Paton's sword and the Howie family tree, spanning nine centuries. The descent of the present tenants is traced to the Huguenots of the Albis area in southern France and the Waldensian Protestant sect which originated in the Piedmont in northern Italy. The aim of the *Trust* is to preserve Lochgoin as a monument to man's for-titude and faith — so glowingly exemplified in the signing of the

44

Covenant in 1638. Stuart King Charles I was petitioned to grant the signatories freedom to continue their worship of God in the presbyterian manner to which they were accustomed. The Covenanters also challenged the King's role as Head of the Church. A facsimile of the Covenant document with the signatures gathered in Greyfriars Kirkyard in Edinburgh is displayed at Lochgoin.

Lochgoin links with Fenwick and Eaglesham rather than Mearns. The neighbouring farms of Highfield and Shieldhill, however, mark the south-east extremity of one of Mearns early postal walking routes. Six days a week, in all weathers

> a nippy wee man Tommy McMeechin left the village before 7 a.m. . . . . fully loaded . . . . puttees on his legs . . . . and went off up the Eaglesham Road, past the houses at Mearnskirk, past Billy Ritchie's smiddy (now New Jasmine House), to East-field, Southfield, Westfield, the Hazeldens, Crook, the Star, Broadlees; down to Muirshiel on the Earn; up to the Moorhouses, Langlee, the Binnen; across the fields to Shieldhill; then half an hour at Highfield for a cup of tea; across the fields again down and up to the Floaks, and on up to High Cairn; down via Low Cairn and Brownside, reaching Loganswell and his last call at Greenhags (now the District Council coup) by mid-day,

whence back to do "a bit of tailoring in the afternoon". In those days there were no days off for Christmas or New Year. On New Year's Day he reached Greenhags about 6 p.m. often with icicles on his beard but warmed by a few more 'teas' than his usual one cup at Highfield.

This tailoring postie was succeeded by Bertie Crawford from Malletsheugh cottages. He "sang all the time" and also covered the hilly round on foot. A bike was of little use for short cuts across the fields and burns. A cycling postie on the Capelrig, Barcapel, Patterton route used to interrupt his deliveries to lay snares, the postbag being handy for bringing back the rabbits caught. Singing, hunting, and tea-drinking posties sadly disappeared with the introduction of vans in the thirties. In the days before broadcasting, when country families read weekly rather than daily newspapers, immediate happenings and urgent communications came through neighbours, children, the postie, itinerant salesmen and tramps. The Lammies of Greenhags heard of the outbreak of the Great War from a tramp at their back door who knew his statement, "The War has broken oot," would be good for something to eat in exchange.

Most of the farmland has now gone — for housing estates and other purposes — and many of the farmhouses and steadings have been demolished or converted into suburban houses. Changed or gone are most of the burns and hedgerows.

Pink dog- roses with glossy hips,
Rambling brambles to stain your lips,
Snow-white hawthorn with crimson haws
That's how the farmers predicted 'snaws'.

Oh, what a glorious place to nest,
Food for the winter, safety for rest,
Free from the predator, protected by thorn,
No better place for your young to be born.

Springtime brings flowers and nectar galore,
Insects and bees buzzing round by the score,
While green caterpillars are munching your leaves
A spider's preparing a meal as she weaves.

Under the branches a nest for a mouse,
While hedgehog and stoat and a shrew find a house:
And deep underground in the roots and the furrows,
Foxes scrape earths and rabbits dig burrows.

Now the surveyor with pencil in hand
With one short report condemns the whole land,
And buildings rise up and a new estate grows
Where once a whole world lived among the hedgerows.

And the crystal-clear burn which sparkled and wound,
Now has been forced into pipes underground,
And no longer meanders and winds through the field,
For to man's selfish acts it must finally yield.

Why didn't they ask?

Someone might have wanted a hedge instead of a fence —
Men are dense —
Or a burn with primroses on its banks and tadpoles in its pools —
Men are fools.

46

This lovely poem is one of an award-winning collection of poems written by Primary 6 pupils of Crookfur School during session 1985/86 for a competition sponsored by the Poetry Society and the World Wildlife Fund. Ted Hughes the Poet Laureate particularly commended another poem, "Now the Old Village is Gone"; it mourns the lost village and all its haunts, a result of the development of the present Shopping Centre.

"They didn't have to put it there," the old man said,
His heart was heavy and his eyes were sad,
The village and the house where he was born,
The cobblestones he played on as a lad,

The baker where he bought his early rolls,
And broken bannocks were a special treat,
The butcher where his mother bought her beef,
Cleaver in hand and sawdust at his feet,

The grocer with his rounds of home-made cheese,
And tins of biscuits open on the shelf,
Weighing his coffee, scooping up his tea,
For here you didn't have to help yourself.

But best of all the Jenny a' things shop,
Where children pressed their noses on the glass,
Crammed to the sill with beads and books and toys,
Socks and laces, ornaments of brass.

"They didn't have to put it there," he said,
"I know a village not so far away,
With *Conservation Village – Please Take Care.*
I was betrayed and banished on that day
They took my home away.
They didn't have to put it there."

Though greatly regretted by its inhabitants, the passing of the Newton village may have been somewhat less lamented by the countryfolk of the parish if the remarks of two Loganswell octogenarians are anything to go by:

47

the Village . . . . och . . . . jist a wee footerie place . . . . two
streets . . . . the country was the place to be living . . . . we had
a hundred and one things to be doing . . . . couldn't tell you
everything . . . . never time to get bored . . . . we were more
contented then.

Some of the countryside has of course survived, and although
afforestation has begun at the Eastwood/Kilmarnock & Loudoun
District boundary, most of the moorland of Christopher North's
MOST GLADSOME PARISH remains much as it has been
for centuries.

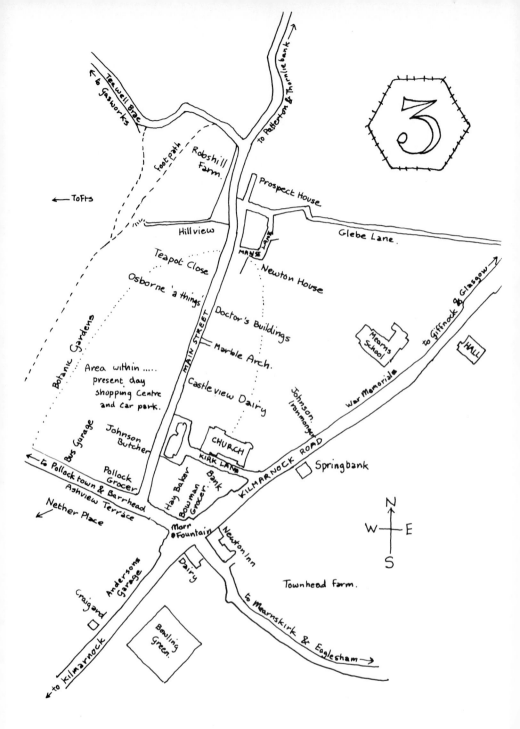

VILLAGE LIFE ...
and WORK

The principal village in the parish is Newtown, situated about
half a mile north west from the parish church. It is a burgh
of barony, and has the right of holding a weekly market, and two
annual fairs. It contains about 500 or 600 inhabitants, and is
formed chiefly of two rows of houses on the Glasgow and
Ayrshire road, with a good Inn.

So wrote the Rev. MacKellar in the *Second Statistical Account*.
One hundred years later – in 1939 – the Rev. Boyd Scott wrote
in "Old Days and Ways in Newton Mearns"

Mearns has lost its isolation; and the village of Newtown is
now little more than a grey smudge upon the great red-roofed
suburbia that has appeared above ground like a coral reef above
the green sea.

A generation on and this "grey smudge" itself has gone. Not a
trace of the old village remains, only a rich seam of memories.
Post-war neglect culminated in demolition in the sixties.

The environs of each of the four roads radiating from the Cross have wholly changed. On the north-east corner stood the principal landmark of the opening decades of this century, Newton Inn, one-time terminus of Porter's bus to Giffnock Station and famous all around for its Friday night dances. The young dancers may have learned their steps at Miss Brodie's dancing classes in Main Street. Opposite Newton Inn on the other side of Eaglesham (then Newton) Road was Burn Cottage, a dairy. Both Inn and Cottage backed on to the fields of Townhead Farm — the neighbouring Townhead House remains — and Mearns Bowling Club bought some Townhead land for its green in 1920. The Club continues to

thrive. Opposite the bowling green and diagonally opposite the Inn was Andersons' Garage, separated from Barrhead (then Newton) Road by a line of houses built right on the street but with gardens behind. Shops with houses above stretched along the north side of Barrhead Road and round into Main Street. In the thirties three further rows of shops were built alongside Ayr (then Kilmarnock) Road. The row replacing the houses which had faced Newton Inn was demolished with the village to make way for the present Shopping Centre; the other have lasted — between the bowling green and the lights, and between the church and the school.

Mearns Cross looking North

Mearns Cross looking South

54

Carrying the inscription "THEIR NAME LIVETH FOR EVER-MORE" the War Memorial honours thirty-nine men from the Parish of Mearns who fell in the Great War and thirty-two who fell in the Second World War. Originally sited in front of Mearns School, a few years ago it was moved to its present attractive location, a focal point in the rose garden adjacent to the bowling green. The rose beds were laid out in their present form in the 1970s by members of Mearns Horticultural Society to commemorate their late president, John Russell, in the tradition of his family a life-long member of the Society, and President from 1945–73. The varieties of roses chosen are Pink Parfait, Piccadilly, Blessings, and Peace – a fitting honour to one of Scotland's famous rose-growers: and equally appropriate as a setting for the War Memorial.

The Rev. MacKellar referred to fairs and a market, but over the last hundred years the only reminders of these events were the Annual Cattle Show held until the 1930s and, still going strong, the Flower Show organised by Mearns Horticultural Society. The following excerpts from the *Centenary Year Book* of the Society characterise Mearns' longest standing recreational institution.

No written record is available of the early years of the Society but it has been said that Mr John Russell, grandfather of the President, calling at the smiddy found some locals arguing about which of them had grown the largest cabbage. At Mr Russell's invitation they each brought their exhibits the following Saturday to his joiner's shop to have them judged. The judge's decision was hotly disputed; they agreed, however, that a competition should be organised with independent judges. This was in 1858. The first Shows were held in the Mearns Inn hall; then in the Old School; then in the Parish Church hall in Ayr Road, where they continued with the addition of marquees and tents overflowing into the ground next door belonging to Mr Brocklehurst, until they returned to the Main Hall of the new Mearns School.

The Mearns Rose Society formed in 1897 was an offshoot of the Horticultural Society . . . . Mr Neil Russell, Secretary, in the Year Book of 1901/2 reported on the great improvement in cultivation locally over the position some four or five years earlier. At the Society's Exhibition held on 20th July 1901 there were classes for Nurserymen, Gardeners and Amateurs, Confined Section, Local Amateur Section, Bouquet and Basket Section for the ladies . . . . Over 1000 rose blooms were on show that day.

In 1940 no prize money was paid to exhibitors – a donation of £75 was made to the Red Cross. When the Society resumed its activities in 1945 it donated £215 to the Welcome Home Fund.

1947 saw the introduction of a Spring Bulb Exhibition, which was promoted primarily for the purpose of widening and encouraging the interest of school children in horticulture.

The spring and summer shows continue with classes for handcrafts, baking, children's art, floral arranging, wild flowers, as well as the traditional garden flowers and vegetables. About twenty trophies are awarded.

Facing the War Memorial and John Russell Memorial Garden, from the beginning of the century until 1980, the most conspicuous landmark was Andersons' Garage, with over 100 employees during its peak years. The oldest document in the firm's archives is addressed to Robert Anderson, Esquire, Cycle Agent, Thornliebank, and reads:

Dear Sir,
Referring to your esteemed enquiry for a secondhand Beeston Humber Tandem, we are pleased to inform you that our customer will accept your offer of £17.
Trusting this will prove satisfactory, and awaiting the favour of your esteemed reply.

Dated 13th November 1899, it came from "The Oldest Established Cycle Depot in Glasgow", Rennie & Prosser Ltd. Half a century on, during the first week of December 1950, over 1700 guests were invited to Andersons' Jubilee Exhibition. Its theme was THEN AND NOW.

The Jubilee display centred on a new Humber Hawk, flanked by two vintage Humbers, a 1903 5 h.p. two-seater and a 1905 10 h.p. four-seater, plus a 1904 Humber motor cycle – all in running order. Five thousand or more spare parts were also on show. The accompanying poster "A Little History and An Explanation" reads:

> The original business of Coal Merchants was founded in Spiersbridge in 1832 by William Anderson, the present Directors' great-grandfather. A grandson, Robert, later branched out into the cycle business. He was himself a keen cyclist and had a number of creditable performances in road events to his name. His keen interest in the internal combustion engine and a natural mechanical aptitude led to the provision of facilities for the repair of mechanically powered vehicles in 1900, the first such to have attention being an Albion belonging to Mr Crebar of Gorbals Waterworks.
>
> The next stage was the establishment of the present premises in Newton Mearns in 1904 and in 1915 our Giffnock branch was opened. These facilities were provided at a time when such places were few and far between, but this farsighted and enterprising policy, and the reputation rapidly acquired by Robert Anderson for thorough workmanship and sound reputable business methods, built up a business which many people were surprised to find in what was, until comparatively recently, a small village . . . .
>
> In 1930 the two firms of William Anderson and Robert Anderson were combined in a private Limited Company, and two years ago the Coal and Contracting Departments were disposed of to enable concentration on the car business.
>
> Humber Ltd celebrated this year the Jubilee of their car manufacture and it is interesting to note that we have been connected with Humber cars from the beginning and are now the oldest Humber distributors. Our connection with Humber Ltd actually goes back before 1900 as we sold Humber cycles before there were any cars. Humber Ltd are now, of course, part of the immense Rootes Group for which we are distributors.

Among many well-wishing messages was the following telegram from Sir William and Sir Reginald Rootes:

We send our congratulations on reaching your jubilee which by happy coincidence falls in the same year as that of Humber Ltd. We are proud of the long and friendly association we have enjoyed together and send you our best wishes for the future.

Coventry, 4/12/50

From a motor trade colleague came a more personal letter (quoted to show the immense changes the firm had experienced since coming to Mearns Cross):

Dear friend Robert,

When I was at your remarkable display last night it occurred to me that the last time I was actually on your premises was 46 years ago — the occasion was a visit with my chief of that time Johnny Matthews who wanted to show off his 3½ h.p. De Dion Voiture to his friend Robert Anderson. We had one engine stop on the way* and that was quite an achievement in those days to travel the distance to Mearns with or without involuntary stops.

My congratulations to you and your brothers on the best Motor Trade Show of its kind that I have ever seen.

I tips my 'at to ye,

Yours aye,

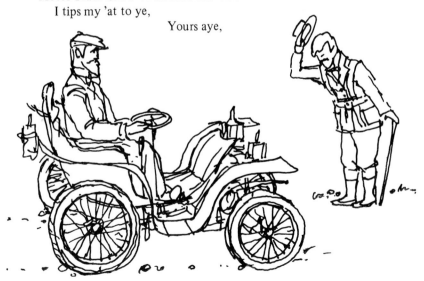

* from the centre of Glasgow.

58

munitions workers

Andersons' business depended upon the sales of new cars; used car deals; and engineering. In this last area the garage had a particularly high reputation. During the War the skills of the Engineering Workshop were re-deployed in munitions manufacture, innovative work being masterminded by James Anderson. His best known invention, patented soon after the War, was the VERTIMAX lathe, the manufacturing rights for which he sold to an American company in the mid 50s, by which time he had come out of the car business to run his own engineering firm in Thornliebank Industrial Estate. As a young man, James Anderson designed and built a four-wheel-drive sports car which pre-dated jeeps. This vehicle is presently on display in Glasgow Transport Museum.

The most flourishing side of the garage business lay in the sales of new cars: Hillmans, Humbers, Sunbeam Rapiers and Alpines. This was, of course, severely affected by the recession in the British Motor industry evident from the early 1960s; and the firm's fortunes inevitably came to depend greatly upon the success of Rootes at Linwood. In the autumn of 1962 Andersons' advertised in the *Evening Times:*

WE ARE PROUD TO PLAY OUR PART IN
THIS GREAT NEW ROOTES VENTURE

For many years we have been closely associated with these fine Rootes products — Humber, Hillman and Sunbeam Cars — and confidently predict an equal success for the new 'Baby' from the Linwood Factory.

We look forward to playing our own part in furthering its future when it is launched out on the world — very soon, we hope!

Best of luck!

IMP SALOON . . . . .   £509.1.3 (£420 + purchase tax £89.1.3)
IMP DE LUXE . . . . . . £533.4.7 (£440 + purchase tax £93.4.7)

Made in Scotland by Rootes Motors Limited.

SEE AND TRY THE HILLMAN AT . . .
ANDERSONS OF NEWTON MEARNS.

Andersons of Newton Mearns as it looked at the turn of the century . . . it was to grow into one of Glasgow's best-known businesses.

Cash flow problems followed the takeover of Humber by Rootes, who closed the two-tier dealer network. In the best years of the fifties Andersons' supplied twenty-two subsidiary dealers in Renfrewshire and north Ayrshire and had 120 employees on their payroll. Market changes, national and international, however, gradually undermined Andersons' wholesale trade in new cars. Retailing had accounted for only 40% of the new car business and it was impossible to increase this sufficiently to compensate. Nor was compensation possible from more turnover in used cars. This line had expanded from 1938 after the stables (previously housing eight horses) and the hayloft were altered and extended to accommodate secondhand cars. With regret, in 1980, but while still in a position to meet their liabilities fully, the fourth generation directors of this family firm announced its closure. The end of an era for many Mearns families.

In the middle years of the century another garage of a very different style was another major employer. Drivers, conductors, conductresses, mechanics and office workers of Western S.M.T. were based at their Newton Mearns depot on the land that is now the west car park of the Shopping Centre, stretching from the Bottle Bank to the Fairweather Hall. This depot is now located in Thornliebank.

Alongside the Bus Garage, in the park was a football pitch with so steep a gradient that the crossbar of the goalposts at the Fairweather Hall end was invisible from the corner flag at the swings end. This part of the park is now Fordyce Court, the design of which takes full advantage of the sloping site. Here the District Council has provided sheltered homes for the elderly: thirty-six flats, guest room, communal lounge, and warden's house — ideally situated within minutes of shops and public transport. They were opened in 1977 by Dr and Mrs William Fordyce. Daffodils given by the Fordyces bloom every spring on the grassy banks between the flats and Capelrig Road.

The name Fordyce is a tribute to forty-eight years of loyal service to the village and surrounding country district by the doctor, who retired in 1974. On his arrival in Mearns in 1926 as assistant to Dr Mackinlay, Dr Fordyce lodged in one of the cottages of Townhead Farm, then behind Newton Inn at the Cross. Thus, a wheel had turned full circle when in 1960 he sold his rooms at 23 Barrhead Road to Andersons' (for £350) and built new consulting rooms at the Cross where the innyard had been. This multi-sided surgery, now extended, is presently occupied by Doctors Wallace, Quin, Marshall and Penney.

Dr and Mrs Fordyce have a fund of tales about Mearns prior to the 'bungalow invasion'. Here are some of their reminiscences and anecdotes:

We lived in Kilmarnock (now Ayr) Road till 1964 in a two-storey house of our own design, built for £1900 on a feu let by the Templetons of Crookfur. Our water supply came from a pipe lead from the private supply of the Hannays of *The Broom*. Our house had neither name nor number until in 1929 the Post Office requested a name for practical purposes so it became 'Craignairn' and some years later the P.O. declared it to be No. 194. A single row of individual houses lined the opposite side of the road and behind these lay fields where we could hear the corncrakes on summer evenings. Our bedroom was at the front and we slept with the windows wide open. In the early morning the milk lorries were the only 'traffic' we recall. Mr Mitchell of the Floak passed each day at 5 a.m. with his milk and if he wanted a visit he put a note through the door, telephones being few and far between in these days. Consultations were also conducted from the bedroom window and calls requested.

"Come quick, doctor, it's Mary!"

"Right, I'll be along — but you've still to pay for the last one you know."

Occasionally unpaid bills were passed to a debt collector and surprising responses could ensue. The following came from Galston:

"Dear Sir, I got the account from the police amounting to ten shillings that you have sent me for John Young but he dozent stop here and I don't know nothing about John Young.
Yours trully John Young."

63

Our own accounts were paid monthly (fairly promptly) in pounds, shillings, pence, half-pence and farthings — florins, half-crowns and ten shilling notes, R.I.P. Both the grocer and the butcher's boys called daily for our order, which was duly delivered by both boys on bicycles with large baskets attached. Bowman (Barrhead Road) and Pollock (Main Street) were rival grocers: both were patients so we gave them our 'patronage' month about.

When we started married life we had a young girl from Lossie-mouth trained for the previous six months by my mother. The word 'servant' had already become unacceptable and 'maid' was also losing favour; by whatever name, however, we employed one at around £3 per month all found, i.e. board, uniform, training, insurance. She usually had two half days per week.

The class structure was simple and direct — until 1939:

1. The Big Houses — Balgray, Barcapel, Todhill, Capelrig, Hazel-dean, Craigend, Fa'side, Netherplace, Greenbank . . .
2. The Farms
3. The Village
4. Last and least, the Bungalow Dwellers on either side of the Kilmarnock Road.

When the Binnan (farm S.E. of Eastwood Golf Course) was being prepared as waterworks a team of Irish labourers was enlisted. On a Saturday night they tended to find their way down to the Malletsheugh. I was called up one night to one such who after the fatigue of toiling back to the huts sat down on the stove, giving me quite a deep burn to deal with . . . . some weeks later the same gentleman again required my services for, returning up the path in hard frost, he wandered on to the frozen burn and had there laid to rest.

Another Malletsheugh regular during the blackout made an almost fatal error. A caring Council had painted a white line at the edge of the pavement and another in the middle of the road for the safety and convenience of patrons and buses. This character was waiting for his bus at the white line in the middle of the road, greatly surprising the driver who, though slowing, inevitably knocked him over. By the time I got there a policeman was already on the scene. "I'm afraid he'll be dead, doctor, the driver hadn't a chance," and a voice came from under the bus, "No, polis, I'm no deid." Nor was he.

During the War, Italian prisoners occupied corrugated iron huts in the fields flanking the Stewarton Road at Patterton and after they were vacated squatters moved in. Each hut was divided to house two families, which promptly increased. One woman had thirteen and when the fourteenth was duly delivered she said to me as I was filling up the missive for codliver oil, orange juice, etc., "Don't put down Burns, doctor; it's Black now." Mildly curious I enquired why she'd parted from Mr Burns. "Oh, doctor, we just felt we'd nothing in common."

A woman in the camp was once bitten by the Co-operative horse and her husband claimed compensation. I met him later looking very prosperous to be informed, "Mind that bite the wife got? We got fifty quid and I put it on a dog. It came in at 50–1 so I bought a key to a house — you're looking at a man of property now."

Routine medical treatment involved bandaging, stitching and 'bottles' rather than pills. Until Jamieson's the chemist opened in the thirties, the doctor did his own dispensing. Babies were born at home and the District Nurse attended the confinements, sending for the doctor only at the critical moment. Nurse Deas, who worked with Dr Mackinlay and with Dr Fordyce, is said to have had to crawl into tinkers' tents at the Humbie to deliver babies — and that after cycling or walking from the village.

Lost with the old village were many intriguing and pictorial names — Ashview Terrace, Botanic Gardens, Hillview, Prospect House, Hope House, Castleview Dairy, Marble Arch, Teapot Close and the Doctor's Buildings. Few of the old names have survived. Robshill Court, however, is named from Robshill Farm whose owner a century ago — Robin Craig — was much respected for his farming abilities as well as being famous for his toddy making. Furthermore, he was Treasurer of the U.F. Kirk and reported as having greeted their new minister, Rev. Morton, thus: "You'll be the new meenister . . . .weel, I'm the Treasurer and without me you can dae neethin'." Even the 'Court' element of Robshill Court is apt, the two tennis courts of Mearns Tennis Club having lain between Robshill farmbuildings and Russell's yard on the west side of Main Street.

The steep hill down from Robshill, officially designated Green-law Road, is traditionally the Teawell Brae. The Tea Well can still be seen at the foot of the brae below the car entrance to Fordyce

Main Street, Newton Mearns

Main Street, Newton Mearns

68

Court and almost opposite the recently developed Teawell Avenue. The story goes that the water from this Well made a better cup of tea than water pumped at the Barrhead Road end of Main Street. The advent of the Bus Garage ultimately caused the clear water to run brown. By this time, fortunately, running water and sewage drainage had long been supplied to the village houses, the benefactor being William Mann of Whitecraigs House. His name was fittingly commemorated by a drinking fountain which made the salient point at the Cross and became a popular meeting place for the village 'worthies' to chat. The widening of the A77 and demolition of the Barrhead properties led to its removal. It now stands forlornly beside the Fairweather Hall.

Prospect House, facing Robshill

The old village houses stood in rows or were built round 'lands'. At the Robshill end of Main Street was a warren of dwelling houses affectionately known as Teapot Close. One theory to explain the name is that these families were near enough to the Tea Well to make it worthwhile to send a child for as little as a teapotful of water. Marble Arch was the imposing name for a square entry into a square courtyard with several dwellings at ground level, stairs up to an open landing with further houses,

Newton House, former U.F. manse

and two more attic houses above that – homes for ten or twelve families, sharing wash-houses and toilets. Teapot Close residents had to go out into Main Street and round Russell's yard to their spotless but somewhat remote toilet accommodation off the lane through to the park by the tennis courts.

The village had, of course, no monopoly of 'good' names. By the works at Netherplace were the Heigh Row and the Laigh Row of cottages; on the old Mearns Road, near the Red Lion Inn, another such row was called Thumba' Ha' (Thimble Hall) because at one time it was occupied mainly by tailors.

All these small settlements were linked by paths – rights-of-way. In the middle years of the century every New Year's Day morning Jimmy McGhee used to walk each right-of-way to ensure its preservation. They remain – or almost remain. One path follows the burn from Netherplace to Tofts, turns up the Teawell Brae, passes Robshill, continues down Glebe Lane and Shaw Road, reaching Shaw luxury flats (once Shaw Farm) by a lane from Hazelwood Avenue which goes round the flats and on to Mearns Road just below the site of Thumba' Ha'. There it meets the erstwhile route from Mearns Kirk to Kirkhill – once Kirk'ilgait, 'gait' in the Scots sense of 'gateway' or 'entry'. For travellers south from Clarkston, Kirkhill marked the first view of Mearns

Parish Church. Nowadays Kirkhill has its own kirk — the Church of Broom, which began as an extension hall-church in 1942.

The village had the usual range of shops and small businesses — grocer, butcher, baker, draper, dairy, ironmonger, cobbler, barber, even a fortune-teller, and prior to the dry poll three public houses: The Boat, Nanny Strang's and Newton Inn. It was a friendly place, some happy memories of which follow:

> When you paid your bill in Pollock's, you'd get a wee poke of sweeties . . . . Mr Pollock always wore a long snowy white apron . . . . boots for the farmers were hanging all around . . . .and sandshoes and ling fish, salted and dry, hung from the ceiling (he'd cut off bits for you) . . . . and paraffin oil round at the side . . . . and bundles of sticks — altogether a different smell from the coffee-grinding smell of Bowman's.

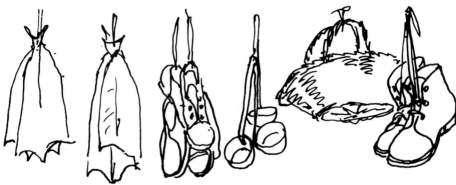

The best rolls ever came from Hay's . . . . you bought them round at the bake-house at the back to enjoy the lovely smell any time from 5 o'clock in the morning . . . . and on Band of Hope nights you hoped to get a fern cake or a pineapple cake as well as a bag of buns.

Another more primitive bakehouse once existed at Mearnskirk, a story of which goes that when the stone sides of the bread oven wore thin, Pate McGee the baker one night went over the wall into the graveyard, collected some big flat stones, and built them into a new oven. His livelihood thus assured, the only snag was that his loaves bore the mirrored imprint "Sacred to the Memory of . . . ."

Johnson's had the best smells — firelighters, carbolic, waxes, oils; and after going up the wide flight of steps into the front shop you could go in and in and in . . . . it was all really mysterious and exciting . . . . an Aladdin's cave.

Along from Pollock's in the wee lane near the Good Templar Hall you could take your laundry for tuppence (2d) get it all mangled . . . . a whole week's wash . . . . you could get a caw at the handle and for a farthing you could buy 'cheuch Jeans' in a poke (toffees that stuck your teeth together).

The Miss Connells in Castle View Dairy at one time carried milk in long-handled cans to their customers every morning. Their shop was never closed, except for two hours on a Sunday morning to enable the two sisters to attend morning worship in the church near-by.

In her front room ———'s mother told fortunes . . . . cards, tea leaves, palm, whatever you liked . . . . she took half a crown a time which was quite dear . . . . folk went all the same.

Next to McCandlish the draper was the doctor's surgery with a row of beautiful green bottles along the window.

At the end of Main Street, next to Teapot Close and Paddy Black's Mission where children came from Glasgow for holidays, was Mary Osbourne's "jenny a' things" shop . . . . if you were prepared to wait she'd have everything . . . . she'd say "If y' jist gie me a meenit till I lay ma han' on it" and she would . . . . cinnamon stick, licorice strap, gobstopper, sherbet dabs – choices galore for a ha'penny.

At the foot of the Teawell Brae were the Gas Works – opposite *Greenside* – run by a Mr Dorward.

When I was young I spent a lot of time in the Gas Works and became a great admirer of Mr Dorward. His was a twenty-four hours a day job, seven days a week, but he had lots of spare time and used to keep hens. He specialised in Brown and White Leghorns. The Gas Works were walled in but he had a hole in the wall at ground level where he could let the hens into the field – by kind permission of my father. It is hard to believe but he used to let the brown hens out first and, after they'd spread out over the nice green grass for a few hours, he could just come to the wall, whistle, and instantly the hens would run for

73

the hole in the wall and back to their house; whereupon, he let the white ones get their turn in the green field.

One of the many attractions for me was when I was allowed to hose down the red-hot char after it had been in the retorts and then drawn out when all the gas had been extracted. It was lovely to see Mr Dorward with his heavy blue shirt open down to his waist shovelling in the new lot of coal. First shovelful to the back, and then not so far, and not so far, shovelful after shovelful till it came to the entrance.

The gable end of the shed where the fires were was part of the boundary wall. On the roadside it was known as the "Hot Wa' " and many a courting couple availed themselves of its comfort on a cold winter's night. In fact I don't think a night in winter would pass without someone using it as a place to cuddle his girlfriend. Lots of children, of course, played around the Hot Wa' as well.

The Directors of the Gas Company used to call to see how things were. They walked down the Teawell Brae to have a word with Willie Dorward and with their coats, hats, gloves, umbrellas and winged stiff collars, they were every inch retired gentlemen with impeccable manners.

There were always carts with pairs of horses and men unloading coal or taking away char and sometimes a farm-cart in for ashes for the farm roads. It was a hive of industry, all hinged on one man.

A family called Porter ran the Inn at the turn of the century and it was really the hub of Mearns . . . . all dances and meetings were held there . . . . three horse buses met the trains at Giffnock Station. There was no Whitecraigs line at that time. The Porters also had horse-driven cabs which travellers could hire to continue to Netherplace or Hazeldean. Gradually the Porters lost the grip of things and the new licensee was A. Guthrie Wren. He moved to East Kilbride after the veto poll — that was sad, since he'd one very beautiful daughter, Nell.

In 1895 when the Caledonian Railway Company were planning the section of their Glasgow/Ardrossan line between Whitecraigs and Neilston, a station was proposed for Mearns — to be located at Tofts below the Teawell Brae. A branch line would deliver coal supplies to the Netherplace Works. Influenced by Sir John Stirling Maxwell, however, the Company laid the line further west, replacing the proposed Mearns Station with Patterton

Station and constructing the present viaduct which carries the line west of the Waterworks to Neilston. Sir John apparently wanted to feu land at Patterton for house building, similar to what he had already done in Pollokshields. The platforms at Patterton Station are very long, having been designed to accommodate crowds of passengers waiting for trains to the city. As an incentive a free feu was offered — on which *Walden* was built, but Sir John's housing ambitions at Patterton were not realised. Not until sixty years later did Patterton become a commuter station.

The results of the railway not coming to Mearns were far-reaching. Coal had to be carted from Whitecraigs or Patterton to all the Works — Tofts, Netherplace, Greenfield and the Gas Works:

> it was a sight always to be seen on weekdays, these magnificent horses with shining harness, hauling those heavy loads of coal up the Ayr Road.

Had there been a more convenient station these works might have expanded; Mearns might have attracted more industry, and might therefore not have become the suburban dormitory it is today.

MEARNS

SCHOOLDAYS

Mearns School was originally in the glebe of Mearns Parish Church. This schoolroom was described with some pride by the minister in 1842 as "one of the largest and airiest of any in the west of Scotland." In it the 103 pupils were taught Latin, geography, arithmetic, English grammar, reading and writing by Mr Jackson, a "very able and excellent teacher", whose annual salary was £34.4/-. Government reports in 1858 and 1860 commended Mr Hunter, dominie from 1847 to 1884, for his teaching ability in Latin, Greek, Mechanics, Algebra and Geometry; while noting that he did not profess Sewing. This skill was taught to the 41 girls by "a female in the village."

old schoolhouse at Mearnskirk (site of present manse)

Mr Hunter became the first Head Teacher in the present school building on Ayr Road, the centenary of whose opening was celebrated in 1976. This milestone in the history of the community was marked by an Exhibition and by the publication of an *Anniversary Magazine*. The cover motif of the magazine

depicts the school badge and the Ayr Road building with its entrance under the bell tower, an entry now walled up. The clock in the tower came later — a gift from Mr Gordon of Netherplace, Chairman of the School Board. With full ceremony and the pupils granted a half day in honour of the occasion, it was started on 1st May 1903. An *Evening Times* article in 1956 about the school concluded:

> The tower is a well-known landmark. Once when the clock stopped, letters and 'phone calls arrived from Ayr, Kilmarnock, Troon and Prestwick advising of the fault. Business men on their way to the city were obviously missing their time check.

Sadly it no longer tells the time and the chimes on the hours are silent.

Mr Gordon also donated a flagpole for the school grounds. On Empire Day each May, when the Union Jack was hoisted, the pupils stood at the salute and listened to an address by the Head. The swing park — with a maypole made from the mast of a ship — was another gift from Mr Gordon to Mearns.

The original school building now houses some of the Infant classes. The turreted schoolhouse is no longer the Head Teacher's home, but the offices of the Community Education Service. The Centenary Magazine of Mearns School was the product of much hard work and research by present and former pupils, staff and wellwishers, coordinated by Miss Marion S. McFarlane, the Infant Mistress. This book shares the aim of the *Anniversary Magazine*, which Miss McFarlane described thus:

> Our aim in producing this magazine was twofold. We knew that there were many people with former connections with Mearns School who would agree with Mr Forbes when he wrote "Mearns School and all its connections mean so very much to me" and we wanted to involve these people in some way in the celebration of our centenary and revive happy memories for them.
>
> We knew too that there are many people living in Mearns today who know nothing of the days when Mearns was a thriving agricultural community with a real village at its heart and a first class school. Perhaps because education is our business we wanted to record as much as we could of the past for our present generation of Mearns pupils and their parents.

I am very grateful to Miss McFarlane, now retired, and to Mr Morrison, Head Teacher since 1970, for allowing me to draw freely from this fine magazine, celebrating the history of Mearns and its young scholars, willing and otherwise.

The School in Ayr Road was built to meet the requirements of the 1872 Scottish Education Act, which legislated for compulsory schooling for all children. Mr Hamilton of *Greenbank*, who became Chairman of the newly formed School Board, provided the site. The foundation stone was laid in 1875 and at a cost of £4,575 the building opened to pupils a year later. About 200 children enrolled. A marble plaque, still on view in one of the rooms in the old building, commemorates the formal opening.

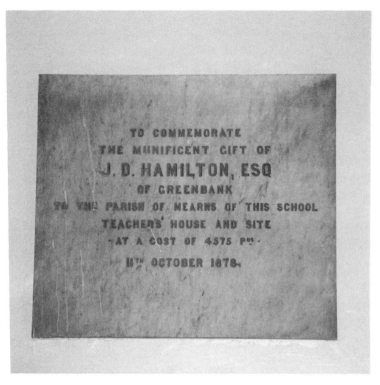

Mr Hunter moved with his pupils from Mearnskirk and continued as Head Teacher until 1884. His responsibilities became more taxing than in the days of volunteers, especially since the staff never totalled more than three or four, at least one of whom would be a pupil-teacher barely older than the senior pupils. In the Log Book on Friday 23rd September 1881 he wrote, "This has been a heartless week of business — so many blockheads to look after", an entry typical of many:

> Great difficulty experienced in teaching a number of both sexes who seem to be incapable of being taught — a most irksome and laborious task.

> A good many defaulters today, some of whom seem impossible to be taught anything — "Verily such a task is a wearing of the flesh."

Great blockheadism displayed by many of the irregular atten-
dants some of whom seem to be retrograding rather than
advancing.

The School Board Officer called today and received a list of
25 defaulters but he refused to visit them on account of the
Board not supporting him so that the delinquents when visited
just laugh at him.

A few of the more lazy pupils absent themselves on a Friday
afternoon in order to get out of the home exercise for Monday
and on Monday they are absent in order to save themselves from
the consequences. The parents are much to blame. I think the
parents connive at this which makes it more difficult to stop.

The great affair for the scholars is the game of football and
a great many of them are more interested in that than any
business of school work.

His daughter, Miss Marion Hunter, who died aged 91 in 1934,
was also a member of staff at Mearns School. After her father's
retiral she served under Mr John Downie, who was Head Teacher
until 1919. By setting the recollections of the late Mrs Jessie
Simpson (nee Currie) against the rules Mr Downie issued to his
teaching staff, it is possible to imagine Mearns school life at the
century.

It was a mile and a half to school [The Currie family lived at
Netherplace.] . . . . we used to leave about eight o'clock in the
morning . . . . we had lots of company . . . . so many children
came from the farms . . . . about a hundred of us . . . .I think
school finished about a quarter to four because we did not get
home until half-past four.
You went in the door under the clock . . . . there was a cloak-
room at the side and a room we called the side-room . . . . then
you went into the big hall which had four classes in it . . . .

82

there was a sliding partition in the centre of the hall and two classes were in each section . . . . Mr Downie's class in one and Mr Fraser's in the other . . . . at the back of the school they had a room we called the back room . . . . there were six classes altogether . . . . there was a coal fire at each end of the big hall . . . . we sat at long benches and we had just planks of wood for seats — no backs or anything fancy like that. The benches were tiered.

All the concerts and Church soirees in the village took place in the school. The partition was opened up and a platform fitted. Everybody went to the concerts. It was a great occasion.

Mr Downie was the Head Master. He had four of a family — all very clever children — Fred, Nan, Nelson and Rhona. Nelson was killed in the First World War a few days before the end of the War. I used to go to parties at their house. I remember I went to five parties one winter, going in from school, and it was great fun. We used to talk about 'old Downie' and some people didn't like him, but of course he would be strict. I liked Mr Downie, I got on fine with him and I liked his family. They were very kind. We had a long walk to school and on a wet day if we got very wet they used to take us into the house. They had a very good maid, Annie Johnstone her name was, who dried our coats and gave us tea. Mrs Downie was very nice and took in any child who got very wet. We were in for a long time and of course we thought it was marvellous — much better than lessons.

Mr Fraser was my teacher in Standard V. I didn't like him. He was a terror for using his strap. I used to get a dozen a day and I was afraid to tell mother at home because she thought it was for lessons and it was mostly for talking and giggling. Mr Fraser always wore a morning coat and when he bent down the coat tail with the strap in it was hanging down. One day one of the boys gently pulled it out of his pocket. At lunch time they all went up into a field at the Cross, made a bonfire and burnt the strap! He did everything to find out who had taken it but no one would tell.

I can't remember much about the lessons but I do know we had a lot to do. We certainly had home-work. We had four sums every night and exercises, and at the weekend we always had a composition to write. It wasn't as easygoing as it is now. I was always disappointed when I did not win the medal. My sister was very friendly with the girls at Malletsheugh Farm. Their mother used to keep a bottle of ink and a pen in a hole in the wall (outside) and all the children met there in the morning and compared their exercises and changed them.

Some of us lived too far away to go home at lunchtime. In the grocer's we could get a glass of milk for a ½d and a bun or roll with treacle for ½d or with syrup for 1d. You could be unlucky and get your syrup spread with the knife from the treacle jar and get a lot of treacle in it. That went on for years until Mrs Brodie in the public house in the Main Street started a tearoom and she made dinners for the school children. She charged 1½d for a one course meal. It was very satisfying.

Everyone went to the local school. The nearest station was Thornliebank or Giffnock. Porter's horse-drawn bus left the Inn at the Cross at a quarter to nine for Giffnock Station and anyone going to town for the day travelled that way. Porter also had cabs for hire. Later the older pupils could go to Glasgow schools as the stations at Whitecraigs and Patterton had opened.

Mr Downie and Mr Fraser were no doubt strict with their pupils when necessary. Mr Downie was certainly strict with his staff. His "Rules for Teachers" are systematically recorded in the official Log Book soon after his appointment.

HOURS:	Teachers must be in school not later than 9 a.m.
TEACHING:	No Teacher is to sit while teaching. Exception Sewing lesson. Classes are not to be left unattended. Pens, etc. can be brought from the Press by a pupil. No unnecessary communication between Teachers during School Hours.
LESSONS:	Children to show books at the beginning of Lesson. All without Books, seams, etc. to be sent to the Head Master every day until they get them. Teachers to prepare lessons for following day (Object lessons to be written out). History and Geography must be hearkened without textbook. The Lessons for the week to be written in Lesson Book on Thursday afternoon.
READING:	Class rooms to be used for the teaching of Style in Reading. All children must point to the word and read with the one who is reading aloud. Repetition of words and careless mistakes to be strictly dealt with.

WRITING:	During Writing Hour a lesson to be given on Blackboard. Date to be placed at end of each day's work.
ARITHMETIC:	Backward children to receive special drill.
DICTATION:	All failures to write 30 words on slates and bring in 15 words on following day.
PUNISHMENT:	Punishment is to be inflicted only on the hand.
REGISTERS:	Registers (Attendance) must be added and checked on Friday afternoon after the dismissal of the children and Total Attendance entered in Register of Summaries . . . . Lines should be drawn and 'Holiday', 'Fast Day' etc. entered immediately after occurrence. Neither Registers nor Fee Lines are to be written out during school hours.

Jessie Currie was one of the names on Mr Downie's earlier Registers; on his later Registers was the name Sam Drysdale. Mr Drysdale was Deputy Head of Mearns School from 1952 to 1964 and in 1976 he contributed memories of his Mearns boyhood to the *Anniversary Magazine.*

Mearns of sixty years ago was still very much a village; separated from the city by green fields and by a fairly laborious journey, it had a character of its own. With its small satellite communities of Netherplace, Tofts, Malletsheugh, Mearnskirk and Hazelden it produced a variety of characters. Nicknames were more commonly used than given names: "The Cod", "The Haddie", "Sneck", "The Duke", "The Wig", "Torry Wull", are but a few; while placenames such as 'The Marble Arch', 'The Teapot Close', 'The Puddock Ford' are colourful examples of the speech of the time.

Although hard work was the rule the pace of things was slower. Traffic on the main road, "The New Line" as it was called, moved at little more than ten miles per hour. The road, deep in mud in winter and dusty in summer, restricted the speed of vehicles (many of them steam-driven) which carried milk to Glasgow from the creameries of Ayrshire.

Going uphill past the school, lorries went at a walking pace and tempted the more adventurous to catch hold and perhaps even mount the tail-board. Once past the Cross a higher speed was reached, but as the road rose towards Malletsheugh it was usually possible to dismount. An added attraction was that such vehicles carried loads such as fruit and lemonade.

The traffic was sparse, however, and going to and from school it was possible to kick a ball from one side of the main road to the other. After school football went on regularly in Barrhead Road against the door of Pollock the grocer's garage. It was here that every boy learnt the arts of football. Only occasionally was the game interrupted by the law. Playing fields were non-existent but farmers' fields provided a good pitch. This could be interrupted by the farmer asserting his rights and many a game ended when 'Gaffer' Craig or 'Eck' Gilmour put a knife through the ball or appropriated the jackets which formed the goalposts.

The school of those days consisted of the present infant block itself consisting of the original 1876 school, the downstairs classrooms, plus the upstairs addition erected early this century. Across the playground was the Cookery Room or Laundry. This was demolished to allow building of the extension of the sixties. The rest of the area was playground spread with ashes, the cause of countless grazed knees. The part of the playground nearest Main Street was grass-covered and open only in summer. Part of this was a school garden tended by the senior boys.

School seemed a secure settled place. Many of the teachers appeared to have been there for ever and went on a long time after that. We knew the rules and the penalties. Justice sometimes was three-tiered, administered by Headmaster, police and parent, although not always in that order. We don't seem to have suffered too much under this system.

Presiding over our playground activities was the janitor, Frankie Corrigan, who sharpened our pencils, tended our cuts and bruises and hauled wrong-doers before the Headmaster. At the intervals football held pride of place and went on constantly summer and winter except for short periods when complaints from adjoining householders forced a halt. Outside of school there was always football.

As boys we also had 'girrs' or 'girds', iron hoops made by one of the local blacksmiths. These were controlled by an iron 'cleek', a hook-like piece of iron. With these we would cover many miles round the country roads and I can still hear the bell-like

ring they made as we raced along. A story of these days tells of the boy who arriving home late made the excuse "I lost my girr so I had to walk home." Bogies or fourwheelers were made from any wheels we could lay hands on and envious eyes were cast on any pram which looked as if it might become available.

The fields, burns and lochs were free to us and we sought frog-spawn, birds' eggs, caught 'baggies' or tried to swim according to the season. In fine weather the whole school would set off on foot for an outing. Pilmuir Dam was a favourite venue. The crocodile would wend its way in orderly fashion to the lochside where for some hours we could play as we pleased before being reformed for the return journey.

In winter time half-days were fairly common as poor clothing and footwear didn't stand up to wet and cold, nor was there a school bus. Our expectations were usually confirmed when some pupil was dispatched to Mrs Jackson's in Ashview Terrace where the teachers had their lunch. To us this was a sure sign that school would end at 1 o'clock.

A fall of snow brought out an assortment of sledges. The back of an old kitchen chair was the commonest model although there were more ambitious efforts owned by children whose fathers were joiners or blacksmiths. In default of anything else the kitchen shovel did passingly well. Our run was usually the hill in what is left of the public park, (now Fordyce Court). The Tea Well Brae running from Main Street down to Tofts could be a veritable Cresta Run, but all too soon, just as we had it in good condition, the roadman was sent to scatter grit on it.

If there was hard frost we slid on Pilmuir Dam or Netherplace Dam, but only the favoured few had skates. When conditions were right the Headmaster, the Banker and other notabilities were to be found at Pilmuir, with the farmers, busy at the Curling.

Of happenings at school some odd events stand out: Armistice Day 1918 when one of the fathers home on leave threw open the classroom door and marched us outside. We were aghast at this flouting of the rules, but out we went to join a procession led by a drummer which marched round the village. When it disbanded we all went home. We turned up at school next day fearing a reckoning to come, but to our surprise things just went on as normal. Sometime in the early 1920s we were assembled in the playground armed with pieces of smoked glass, the occasion being a total eclipse of the sun. For once on such occasions the weather was perfect and to a running commentary from the Headmaster the whole process was observed.

By the early 20s a new Headmaster has assumed office — Dr McLaren, who in his 90th year from retirement in Ayr, sent good wishes to Mearns School on its centenary. He recalled his appointment in 1919, from 161 applicants, after being demobilised following three years' War service in France.

The special inducement was an increase in salary from £180 to £300 per annum. I felt a great thrill when I took over the reins those many years ago. In 1920 I organised on my own initiative a Higher Grade Department and in 1923 the passes in the Inter-mediate Certificate were 100%. Pupils from Mearns now entered the 4th year in Shawlands Academy or Glasgow High School. In the latter a special prize in Modern Languages was won by Mearns boys in successive years.

Two of our boys played football for Glasgow Schools v. Liverpool Schools and the Mearns School team won the Glasgow Southside League.

Frank Corrigan was the janitor in these days, followed later by Matthew Raeburn. I still recall the attack by the cleaning staff on Friday evenings. Nothing but perfection was good enough. Put Frank Corrigan in a uniform and the Headmaster need have no worry about discipline in the playground.

One of Dr McLaren's Higher Grade pupils was John Anderson, who later taught at Mearns, Eaglesham and Giffnock Schools before his appointment as Head Teacher of Woodfarm High School on its opening in 1962. Here are some of his recollections of Mearns School at the end of the Great War under the regime of Dr McLaren.

I REMEMBER

Major Smith, late of the Indian Army, who gave us physical training in the playground.

Mrs Raeburn's soup kitchen in the Cookery Room — a bowl of soup and a hunk of bread for a penny.

Armistice Day when the parents came and took us all out of school.

Morning Assembly with Dr McLaren leaning over the rail at the end of the hall to see if Miss Maver had arrived to play the piano.

The hen-house we built in the field for Dr McLaren's hens. Old ham boxes were used.

The arrival of the first Mearns School Badge introduced by Dr McLaren.

The holiday we had when Dr McLaren's first child was born and our hope that he would have a large family.

The first real school sports with running lanes, etc. held on the ladies' hockey pitch at Crookfur.

Hugh Leitch, strict disciplinarian and devoted teacher, later Head of Eaglesham School.

Higher Grade pupils with Dr McLaren's first child

The year John Anderson was Dux and left for Glasgow High School was the year another enthusiastic Mearns F.P., Bill Forbes, started.

It is a wee while now since I attended Mearns School (1923–32) and changed though it may be building wise, the original classrooms are still there and what memories they have for me.

The first person that comes to mind was the 'jannie', Grandpa Corrigan as he was known to one and all. He was a man we all respected and you could go to him with all your many complaints and find a sympathetic ear. He was the greatest pencil sharpener you ever saw; with his old tobacco knife he could give your pencil the longest and sharpest point, and his every free moment seemed to be spent doing this.

Dr Thomas McLaren was the Headmaster – what a man – strict but fair, and could he swing that belt. I should know because I was on the receiving end of it many times. He had developed the habit of always looking above his head before going into his back swing, the reason being he had once broken a light fitting during a belting session. On being told of the Headmaster's Ph.D. we were warned not to approach him with our physical complaints as he was not that kind of doctor.

We had at Mearns, long before school meals came into being, a soup kitchen where for a penny you got a huge bowl of 'tattie soup' made in the copper boiler in the Science Room at the rear of the school by Grandpa Corrigan's daughter Kate. I must admit to the fact that I always attempted to head the queue and then run home for my dinner – aye, that soup was good.

Gibby Graham, the Maths and Science teacher, also doubled as the school football team manager. One of the highlights of the football season was when we assembled in the 3rd year class on Friday at 12.45 to select the team for the following morning.

We were proud of Mearns School and it was during the period when I was there that the school badge was designed as it is now – Mearns Castle.

Dr McLaren left Mearns to become the Director of Education for Moray and Nairn. His successor was Mr Thom, who I remember was most keen on the School Choir. His energies and enthusiasm in this sphere were rewarded when at Greenock

Town Hall the school choir won the Alston Trophy. We were in receipt of high congratulations from the adjudicators and I remember we sang "Hans' Old Mill" and "Which is the Way to London Town?" with a solo from Nora McDermott.

My mother (Jeannie Waterhouse) was a pupil of Mearns and she instilled in us the fondness of Mearns which she held so dearly. My grandfather (Daniel Waterhouse), who was an amateur ornithologist, presented to Mearns School many glass cases containing stuffed birds. I could go on and on as I admit that Mearns and all its connections mean so very much to me. I hope that all of you who have come through Mearns School have acquired a similar liking for it as no doubt there is much truth in the phrase "school days are happy days".

All the best to Mearns School — carry on with the good work.

Mearns school and life in Mearns appealed greatly to the family of the new Head, Mr Thom, one of whom is quoted as saying, "It was like coming to Heaven." Change, however, was all around. New houses were built — N.E. of the Cross covering the area bounded by Ayr Road, Firwood Road, Hazelwood Avenue and Eaglesham Road; and S.E. of the Cross, up the Lanrig Road — Arthurlie, Gilmourton and Raeside Avenues were called after the farming families of Townhead and Maidenhill.

With the opening of Eastwood Senior Secondary School in 1937 (now Williamwood High School), pupils on Higher Grade courses no longer had to travel to Shawlands Academy. Junior Secondary Education, however, continued in Mearns School until Woodfarm opened in 1962.

Under Mr Thom, school work, choir, football, gardening, the annual Bank of Hope Temperance Lecture, theatre outings et alia continued smoothly. Electric lighting throughout the school was installed in August 1936. Another 'bright' innovation was supplying 95 pupils with hyacinth bulbs to grow for a Bulb Show in the spring.

93

1939, however, had entries of a very different style in the official Log:

2nd & 3rd FEBRUARY:	School closed to allow teachers to take part in the Survey under Government Evacuation Scheme.
4th MAY:	Architect examined building with a view to arranging for Protection against Air Raids.
11th SEPTEMBER:	School reopened after being delayed for one week owing to outbreak of War.

WARTIME COMINGS....
and GOINGS

THE ARRIVAL OF THE GLASGOW EVACUEES

Day 1. Saturday

A glorious day in September 1939. That was just as well as there were small groups of evacuees from St Alphonsus' in London Road dotted all over the school playground. We had double the number we had been told to expect as those intended for Busby School (also in Mearns Parish) arrived here too.

The famous 'Panic Bus' had last minute evacuees, expectant mothers – the lot.

There was Mrs Viola with nine children and they all wanted into the same billet! – "Mr Dollan said we'd be OK here!"

Gradually the numbers dwindled as children were taken to various houses – except the hard core – including the expectant mothers. One 'very expectant' was lodged in Mr Thom's room but thought she could "haud on tae the morn".

Later in the day frantic Mearns fathers were searching Shawlands and elsewhere for Dettol – their wives were hysterical and their children lousy.

The hard core were billeted in the Infant rooms on straw palliasses for the night and a field kitchen was set up, manned by Miss Buchanan and Miss Mackenzie. Come morning the rooms and palliasses were crawling; teachers' desks were broken open and rifled; everything had to be burned.

Day 2. Sunday

There were many complaints from the billets about destruction, etc. Having been fitted with new clothes some children disappeared back to Glasgow to show themselves off. They returned next day – lousy again.

The hard core were taken to Fingleton Mill*. Charlie Thom (the Headmaster's son) and a friend volunteered to stay with them – a ghastly experience.

The Glasgow staff took over the staffroom. Our staff were in the school-house.

Day 3. Monday – the first teaching day

There were over 80 in the Infant Room – at desks, on floor and on window-sills. Miss Ritchie and staff were trying to cope when three Lady H.M.I.s arrived complete with khaki knitting to interview Miss Ritchie about what she was doing. They were told to GET OUT.

These abruptly changed days for Newton Mearns were crisply and vividly recollected in 1976 by Miss E.A. Calder for Mearns School's *Anniversary Magazine.* Miss Calder joined the staff in January 1938 and retired in June 1971, thus working with four of the school's seven Heads and perhaps seeing more changes than any other member of staff. When asked for her outstanding memory, her immediate reply was "The Evacuation".

The outbreak of War delayed the re-opening of the school for a week. On opening day, 11th September 1939, about 100 children who had previously attended Glasgow schools enrolled; and in subsequent sessions the school roll fluctuated month by month by hundreds, an organisational nightmare for Mr Thom and his staff. As his second wife later wrote for the *Anniversary Magazine*:

---

* Fingleton Mill had been refurbished in the 1920s in a project for the unemployed organised by Govan Parish Church under the Rev. George McLeod. Ideals and practices first tried at Fingleton were later realised in his Iona Community work.

The change was cataclysmic. From Glasgow came youngsters who had scarcely, if ever, seen green fields or heard the songs of birds and smelt the fragrance of flowers. All these children had to be housed and educated in a wee quiet village. The school was overwhelmed. Every available hall in the district was put to use: even the ground floor of the schoolhouse was utilised.

Green fields, bird song and fragrant flowers were no substitute for fish suppers and the cinema. "Nae fish 'n chips . . . . Nae picturs . . . . ahm gaun hame" was the cry in many a home, especially from the young mothers who had been evacuated with their babies and younger children.

His Majesty's Inspectors officially reported:

The church halls are in use in addition to the school. At the beginning of the session 1939–40 the roll was raised from 471 to 776 by the arrival of the Roman Catholic evacuees. Most of these soon returned to their home area and, while other evacuee children have since been admitted, departures have succeeded arrivals and there has been a decline from the peak figure mentioned to the present total of 575. From the first, the evacuees under the Government Scheme were classified separately and taught by their own teachers. The recall of teachers, however, has not kept pace with the return of children and for a long time two teachers have been wholly engaged with very small groups. Attendance has not been more than moderately good.

Valuable contributions have been made to War Savings and food production has received support. The facilities of the soup kitchen which was initiated some years ago for the benefit of children who travel from a distance were extended to cover the evacuees and in this way a measure of relief has been brought to local householders.

Session 1944–45 H.M.I.'s Report noted a decrease on the roll "mainly by the return of evacuees, from 575 in 1942 to 393 in 1945."

In addition to Wartime Savings, the school supported national collection weeks:

WARSHIPS WEEK – April 1942 – £840 raised
WINGS FOR VICTORY – May 1943 – £1,465.2.4 raised
SALUTE THE SOLDIER – May 1944 – £2,001.2.10 raised

Alongside such special events and an occasional Air Raid Alert, normal schoolwork continued from day to day. A milk scheme was introduced in May 1941, the Log Book later recording "Received Permit from Food Control Committee to purchase 91 gallons, 5 $^{1}/_{3}$ pints of milk weekly." Each autumn the older boys did potato lifting on the local farms. Demonstrations of Wartime Cookery were arranged; a Channel Island evacuee won a nation-wide competition for cooking a simple meal. February 1943 found the teachers engaged in some awkward sewing when 128 pairs of sandshoes arrived – all black, loose, and in one huge random bundle with laces enclosed and thick red thread for the teachers to sew the sizes on each shoe once they had been matched and sorted into pairs. A key listed ten pairs at size 1, fourteen at size 2, fourteen at size 3, twenty at size 4, eleven at size 5, twenty at size 6, three at size 8, eight at size 10, eight at size 11, ten at size 12, ten at size 13 = two hundred and fifty six shoes to sew! Their use, once children's feet were fitted to the sandshoes, must have been fairly limited since – with evacuee classes in the church halls – if the weather was inclement, only a narrow corridor within the school remained for 'drill'.

Mearns escaped direct enemy action. The nearest target areas lay along the River Clyde seven and more miles away . . . .

> not too far away of course to know when something was going on and when it was pretty bad . . . . they bombed the river . . . . it would be a clear moonlit night . . . . very clear . . . . you knew things were dropping . . . . you could see signs of action in the sky . . . . and hear shrapnel dropping, very little though . . . . I remember we'd go out into the open street to see what was happening . . . . curiosity drew you out . . . . you chatted about it and speculated if you could see anything . . . . . it was probably a bit foolish to go out, but any danger seemed far away . . . .

So ran a Mearns-based recollection of the kind of night Clydebank and Greenock were hit. In 1941 civilian deaths in Britain from enemy bombing approached 20,000: over one thousand of these being the result of the blitz on Clydebank on 13/14th March. The previous year had also been bad for Britain with 24,000 dead, half in London.

A DEPARTURE . . . .

AND UNEXPECTED RETURN

In such circumstances it is not surprising that many families concerned about the safety of their children took advantage of the evacuation liners which sailed to Canada and the United States. In the first week of August 1940, for instance, three liners of child refugees reached Canada and two New York. At the end of that same month the Dutch liner 'Volemdam' left the Clyde with over 300 evacuee children on board, including two brothers from 76 Larchfield Avenue. The younger boy withstood an amazing ordeal, which almost a year later was featured in *The Bulletin* of Thursday May 15th, 1941:

"I prayed to God for Help"

SCOTS BOY LEFT BEHIND IN SINKING SHIP

Eleven year old Robert Wilson, the little Scots boy who, it can now be revealed, was left behind on the sinking evacuee ship VOLEMDAM in the Atlantic last August, while his older brother and scores of other boys and girls were safe in lifeboats many miles away, believes that he was saved ultimately because God answered his prayer for help.

Robert was asleep in his cabin when a torpedo struck the ship. In the confusion he slept on, but awoke some time later to find his cabin empty and his little friends gone. He ran on deck and peered out to sea in the slowly darkening night. Not a lifeboat was to be seen. They had left the ship some hours before.

Fell on Knees

"I went down on my knees and prayed to God," said little Robert last night in his house at Larchfield Avenue, Newton Mearns, near Glasgow, when recalling his adventure. "I asked God to protect all the other boys and girls who had got away in the lifeboats, and then I asked Him to help me. A choking feeling came up into my throat, so I went straight back to bed to sleep and forget what had happened. I was alone and terribly lonely.

"In the morning, to my surprise, the boat was still afloat. I ran upstairs again on to the deck. There was a destroyer lying alongside and I shouted until those on the destroyer could hear me."

Not Alone

But someone else heard the boy — one of the members of the skeleton crew who had been left on board the torpedoed VOLEMDAM in an effort to try to save the vessel and bring her to port if possible. He came up on deck and found the boy shouting to the crew of the destroyer.

"I thought all night I was alone on the ship," continued Robert. "I was terribly surprised when I discovered there were several members of the crew on board. They were very kind to me. They played all kinds of games, and gave me anything I asked for. They even secured a lump of the torpedo which plunged into the ship's engine-room and gave it to me as a souvenir."

The VOLEMDAM was towed to a West of Scotland port and the night after his nightmare adventure, Robert joined his mother and father and brother in Glasgow. "I wouldn't like to go on the voyage again, unless Mummy was going with me," he said last night.

Mr and Mrs Wilson, needless to say, made no further plans for their sons to leave Mearns for the duration of the War.

MYSTERIOUS STRANGER

Perhaps the most famous uninvited guest to arrive in Britain this century was Rudolf Hess — who dropped in by parachute as darkness fell on the evening of Saturday May 10th, 1941. He landed on farmland between Mearns and Eaglesham. His Messerschmidt 110 evaded two Hurricanes sent up by Coastal Command in Northumberland and a Defiant from RAF Prestwick before its solitary occupant rolled it over, ejected, and left the plane to crash. Ploughman David McLean found this German pilot entangled in his parachute and from his cottage, Home Guardsmen Robert Gibson and Jack Paterson took 'Oberleutnant Alfred Horn' into custody, imprisoning him at Giffnock Police Station prior to transfer to Maryhill Barracks.

This first capture of an enemy officer of obvious high rank aroused great local excitement — even before the news of his real identity was disclosed the following Tuesday. To have had the Deputy Fuehrer, Number 3 of the Third Reich, in their hands, however briefly, understandably became a source of considerable pride for the 1st District of Renfrewshire's Home Guard Command. Coincidentally, on the second day of the newsbreak on Hess (prisoner, refugee, envoy, traitor, or whatever), *The*

Bulletin carried a front-page tribute from King George VI to the Home Guard on the occasion of its first birthday.

> *I heartily congratulate the Home Guard on the progress made by all ranks since it was established a year ago today. They have already earned the gratitude of their fellow citizens for the prompt and unstinted assistance which they are constantly giving to the Civil Defence services. The Home Guard stands in the direct line of various bodies of Militia, trained bands, fencibles, and volunteers, the records of whose fine spirit and military aptitude adorn many a page of our history.*
>
> *I thank them for the service which they freely give at considerable sacrifice of leisure and convenience, and I am confident that, in cooperation with their comrades-in-arms of the field army, they will fit themselves to meet and overcome every emergency, and so make their contribution to the victory which will reward our united efforts. [14.5.41]*

The Russell family at Newton House heard the news of the capture from their neighbour Mr Thom, Mearns School Headmaster (1931–1945) and Home Guardsman, as Miss Isa Russell recalled:

> We heard the plane, of course, but only Elizabeth saw it. She was seeing off Willie McLaren (later her husband) and they watched it from the front garden. That was why she'd been out so long – so she claimed!
>
> Then on the Sunday afternoon, over our garden wall from the schoolhouse garden climbed Mr Thom in his Home Guard uniform, gun and all – he was going on duty – to tell us that the previous evening late a German plane had crashlanded at the Floors and a senior German officer been picked up by the duty Home Guards. On being asked why such an officer was likely to have flown so far from his homeland, Mr Thom's explanation was crisp and unforgettable. "The rats always leave the sinking ship" were his words. That sufficed.

The characterisation of Captain Mainwaring in "Dad's Army" was soundly based. The low-flying plane had been widely noticed in the stillness of that summer evening. Another ear-witness was Mrs Jean Fordyce:

> We remember the night well. Friends had come in and although it was still light we had already put up the black-out as it took so long. We heard the thrum of a low-flying aircraft and had we looked out we would also have seen it. Sadly we did not.
>
> However next day the doctor was over at Floors Farm. He said to Mrs Baird, "I hear you had a German officer drop in on you last night." She said, "Yes, I was just going up to bed at the time and I saw a white thing on the hedge. I thought I'd left my bleaching out and went back down as the men came in and said, 'It's a German in a white uniform.' 'Oh,' I said, 'is that it?' and went back to bed."
>
> Scots phlegm! I always tbought it would have made wonderful propaganda in the German camp.

The British Government maintained a very low profile on so mystifying an event. Not until 11.20 p.m. on Monday 12th May was official word issued that Hess was in British hands. The communique from No. 10 Downing Street read:

> Rudolf Hess, Deputy Fuehrer of Germany and Party Leader of the National Socialist Party, has landed in Scotland under the following circumstances:—
>
> On the night of last Saturday an Me 110 was reported by our patrols to have crossed the coast of Scotland and to be flying in the direction of Glasgow. Since an Me 110 would not have the fuel to return to Germany, this report was at first disbelieved.
>
> Later on an Me 110 crashed near Glasgow with its guns unloaded. Shortly afterwards a German officer who had baled out was found with his parachute in the neighbourhood suffering from a broken ankle. He was taken to a hospital in Glasgow where he at first gave his name as Horn, but later he declared he was Rudolf Hess.

He brought with him various photographs of himself at different ages, apparently in order to establish his identity. These were deemed to be photographs of Hess by several people who knew him personally. Accordingly, an officer of the Foreign Office, who was closely acquainted with Hess before the War, has been sent up by aeroplane to see him in hospital.

At 2 a.m., following a telephone call to Glasgow from Churchill and Eden in London to their Foreign Office representative, Mr Ivone Kirkpatrick, the Ministry of Information announced:

The identity of the man who landed from a Messerschmidt in Scotland – as mentioned in the communique from No. 10 Downing Street last night – has now been established beyond all possible doubt as Rudolf Hess.

A revelation, indeed, for the pressmen of the world, adding fuel to the information which had been transmitted earlier that Monday evening by the wireless of the Third Reich:

On Saturday May 10th at about 6 p.m. Rudolf Hess set off on a flight from Augsburg, from which he has not yet returned . . . . suffering from a mental disorder . . . . victim of hallucinations . . . it must be considered that party member Hess either jumped out of his plane or has met with an accident.

Indeed he had jumped out of his plane, 940 miles N.W. of Augsburg and within a few miles of his destination – from a technical and navigational point of view a remarkable flight. Hitler's hopes that his loyal friend had drowned in the North Sea were shattered within hours. The Nazi propaganda machine had a busy week ahead issuing a series of statements to salvage as much credibility within the Reich as possible after the embarrassing news of the Deputy Fuehrer's safe arrival in Britain had been broken to the world by British-based journalists and political commentators. The story more or less emerges from that week's headlines. The following are from *The Glasgow Herald* and *The Bulletin.*

Tuesday 13th May

HITLER'S DEPUTY FLIES TO GLASGOW IN STOLEN PLANE

RUDOLF HESS PARACHUTES FROM CRASHED FIGHTER

AMAZING SEQUEL TO BERLIN STORY OF 'SUICIDE'

THE FLYING REFUGEE

Wednesday 14th May

GLASGOW MIGHT EXPECT RAIN OF BOMBS

PREMIER REVEALS LITTLE NEW CONCERNING HESS

BULLET HOLES IN TAIL OF HESS'S PLANE

FORMER NAZI CHIEF TELLS WHY HESS FLED

WORLD'S LIMELIGHT ON SCOTS

HESS CHATTED TO HOME GUARDS

FIRST SPLIT IN NAZI PARTY

Thursday 15th May

HESS TELLING LONG STORY AND 'TALKING FREELY'

HESS'S QUEST FOR A SCOTS DUKE

HESS FLEW TO MEET DUKE OF HAMILTON

CHURCHILL MAY NOT SEE HESS

PUT HESS IN DOCK SAYS CIVIC CHIEF

HESS ADMITS TO TYRANNY IN GERMANY

Friday 16th May

BERLIN DENOUNCES NAZI EX-CHIEF

PREMIER DID NOT BELIEVE IT WAS HESS

'SENSATIONAL DOCUMENT' EXPECTED

HESS REPORT BEING PREPARED FOR MR CHURCHILL

HESS FEARS FOR GERMANY, BBC TELLS THE NAZIS

Saturday 17th May

PREMIER DELAYS REPORT ON HESS

Events of the War gradually pushed the Hess news off the front pages but speculation remained – and remains even yet.

Hess was first confined at Buchanan Castle, Drymen; then taken secretly to the Tower of London; and finally imprisoned elsewhere in Britain until 6th October 1945. The outcome of his trial as a war criminal at Nuremberg was the life imprisonment sentence which he is still serving in Spandau Prison, West Berlin, under rotating Soviet, French, British and American military guard. *

In May 1941 with so few facts available, relative silence from the British Government, and reports from Germany of insanity, speculation was rife. May 18th's *Sunday Post* front page article was not untypical:

HESS – BIRD, RAT, OR GIANT PANDA?

Speakers yesterday differed in their opinion of Rudolf Hess – but they agreed he was a strange animal.

Lieutenant-Commander Fletcher, Parliamentary Private Secretary to the First Lord of the Admiralty, said at Cleethorpes that a very strange bird had arrived in Scotland. Hess may be a swallow or a cuckoo, but one swallow does not make a summer, and the cuckoo, in spite of the simple and ingenuous notes of its call, has a sinister side to its character.

Mr Herbert Morrison, Home Secretary and Minister of Home Security, said – "It doesn't matter which kind of animal Hess is. Whether he is Rat No. 1 or a Trojan Horse or just a Giant Panda over here in the vain hope of finding innocents to play with, the main thing is he is caged." Mr Morrison added that he had no Hess guess, but Hitler's right-hand man, "like the rest of them, was a brutal thug whose hands, like his master's, are stained with some of the worst political crimes of modern times."

---

* Died August 1987.

Curiosity about Hess's motivation and role took second place, of course, to security. The prudence of disclosing where Hess had landed caused some alarm that Glasgow and the Clyde might again become bombing targets. The Lord Provost of Glasgow, Sir Patrick Dollan, sent a telegram to Mr Ernest Bevin, Minister of Labour and National Service, supporting his efforts to have Hess tried as a criminal and endorsing his protest at a tendency in some quarters to make a hero of Hess. "If such a trial took place," proposed Sir Patrick, "the jury should consist of 12 men representing bombed-out families in Clydeside, Coventry, Liverpool and Birmingham, who would be relied upon to see that justice was meted out to one who has been responsible more than anyone else – excepting Hitler – for their misfortunes."

Sir Patrick's anxiety was equally felt in Parliament. M.P.s were concerned at the official silence of His Majesty's Government, a silence sharply contrasting with the world-wide speculation reported daily in the newspapers and broadcast on the wireless. At Prime Minister's Question Time in the House of Commons on Tuesday 13th May, Mr Churchill was asked if he had "any further statement to make with regard to the announcement that Rudolf Hess, the Nazi leader, had landed in Scotland?"*

The Prime Minister: I have nothing to add at present . . . . but obviously a further statement will be made in the very near future concerning the flight to this country of this very high and significant Nazi leader.

Question: In view of the German propaganda statement over the wireless that this gentleman was suffering from mental instability, has the Prime Minister any information on that matter?

The Prime Minister: . . . after an examination has been made I will make a further statement.

Question: Will my right honourable Friend consider asking the Minister of Information, if necessary, to see that this piece of news is handled with skill and imagination?

* cf. HANSARD Volume 371.

The Prime Minister: .... I think this is one of these cases where imagination is somewhat baffled by the facts as they present themselves.

Question: Will the Prime Minister bear in mind this "gentleman's" record of devotion to the evil genius of Europe?

The Prime Minister indicated assent.

Question: .... Was it prudent to announce that Hess was in a a Glasgow hospital? Was not that rather unfair on the people of Glasgow who may now expect a rain of bombs?

The Prime Minister: Perhaps he will not always be in Glasgow.

Thursday 15th May's Question Time was in a similar vein. Two of the many questions are quoted to show Mr Churchill's cautious replies.

Question: Does not my right honourable Friend consider that it was unfortunate that 48 hours were allowed to elapse during which the enemy were enabled to issue an entirely deceitful version?

The Prime Minister: It was certainly not unfortunate, and if it had been unfortunate, it would have been unavoidable, because we had first of all to establish the identity of the German airman who had landed: and we only had evidence which, though it was very interesting, could not be considered conclusive. In view of the surprising character of the occurrence, I did not believe it, although I was very interested, when I was told in the course of Sunday; but I immediately sent up an officer who knew the Deputy Fuehrer and who was able to speak with him in good and fluent German. While that was still proceeding there came the German announcement of the insanity of the Deputy Fuehrer and his flight to England (*Hon. Members:* Scotland). Yes, Scotland. What had hitherto been a surmise built on increasing probability merged into definite certainty.

Question: Is there any truth in the inference given by the German wireless that they wished to impress upon Germany that Scotland was ready to make a separate peace with Germany?

The Prime Minister: Whatever delusions may exist, that is not among them.

109

Why, however, had Hess flown to the West of Scotland? To do so required extra fuel tanks and he had deliberately prepared his Messerschmidt for this journey of almost 1,000 miles. Hess had a clear destination in mind and calculated accordingly. Among the questions he put to the first Scots he met was one concerning the proximity of their farm cottage to Dungavel. *The Bulletin* of May 15th reported:

> When in the gathering dusk Hess landed at Newton Mearns, Renfrewshire, eight miles from Glasgow, the first thing he asked David McLean, the ploughman who assisted him out of the parachute harness, was the way to Dungavel. He had mistaken a large house which he had sighted as the mansion he was seeking. Hess told Mr David McLean, the Newton Mearns ploughman, that he had information to give the Duke of Hamilton that would be of great use in overthrowing the tyranny that now prevailed in the Reich.
>
> He also stated that great distress prevailed in Germany as a result of the heavy bombing raids by the RAF. He said he had made the most painstaking preparations for his flight from Germany. (The fact that he landed only a few miles from the Duke's mansion proved that it was no haphazard job.) He said that when the Duke was Marquis of Douglas and Clydesdale he knew him well, and that he had flown to Scotland and made his estate his objective, as he had valuable information to give the Duke.

(Text continues on page 113.)

RUDOLF HESS
The Bulletin

27th Year.—No. 114.   **and SCOTS PICTORIAL**   One Penny.

[Registered at G.P.O. as a Newspaper.]   Tuesday, May 13, 1941.   *To-day's Wireless—Page 7*

The 'Plane He Flew

Above—The wreckage of the 'plane in which Hess landed in Scotland.

Right—A ploughman and his mother, who were the first people to meet the Nazi leader.

Sunday "Bag" Now Up to 9

Nine enemy raiders were destroyed on Sunday night, it was established yesterday.

There was little enemy air activity over this country during daylight yesterday. Early in the morning bombs were dropped at a point on the South-East Coast but did little damage and caused no casualties.

Ploughman 'Captured' Hess

"SO we had a distinguished visitor after all," said Mrs M'Lean, mother of the ploughman who "captured" Hess.

just in front of the M'Lean's cottage.

When he came to earth darkness was just closing in on the countryside.

All over the surrounding district people had seen and heard

M'Lean suddenly stood over him and demanded—"Who are you? What are you doing here?"

Without showing any signs of fright or anxiety to escape the airman spoke to him in almost

IN GLASGOW

Parachute Jump After Flight from Germany

L EAVING behind a farewell note, Rudolf Hess, Hitler's deputy, has fled from Germany and is now in a Glasgow hospital suffering from a broken ankle, caused when he parachuted from a crashing Nazi fighter to land near a farm.

Mr David M'Lean, a ploughman at the farm, identified Hess as the man who "fell from the skies" from photographs shown him last night by "The Bulletin." The 'plane, before it crashed, had been seen and heard by people in th surrounding district.

"Suicide," said Berlin

The most amazing story of the war was told late last night in a communique from 10 Downing Street a few hours after Berlin had attempted to anticipate the news by hinting that Hess had left a note showing traces of mental disorder, and had either committed suicide or fallen from a 'plane.

Hess brought photos of himself at different ages to establish his identity, and has been recognised by several people who knew him well. A Foreign Office official has flown by 'plane to see him in hospital.

Mr Duff Cooper, Minister of Information, was present at the Ministry of Information last night when this remarkable announcement was read to representatives of the world's press in an atmosphere of tense drama.

The earlier German announcement was appparently an attempt by the Nazis to break the news to the Germans that Hitler's "shadow" and successor designate after Goering had disappeared.

Flying Towards Glasgow

The Berlin statement said that Hitler had ordered the arrest of Hess's adjutants for not preventing or reporting his flight, and there are repeated attempts to suggest that Hess is suffering from mental disorder.

"On the night of Saturday the 10th," said the statement from 10 Downing Street last night, "an ME 110 was reported by our patrols to have crossed the coast of Scotland and flying in the direction of Glasgow. Since an ME 110 wou'd not have the fuel

HESS HAD BIG HOLD ON HITLER

H ESS, a man of imposing presence, tall, well-built, and with intense commanding eyes, was one of the Nazi old guard.

Although he has never played in open part in the Nazi Cabinet in the way of a Goering or a Goebbels, he had a great influence over Hitler.

On September 1, 1939, day of the German invasion of Poland, Hitler declared to the Reichstag— "Should anything happen to me then my successor is Field-Marshal Goering, and after him party member Hess, to whom you would then owe your duty as leader just as you do to me."

Born In Egypt

"The man who saves Germany," he wrote in his student days "will certainly also be a dictator, but in sacred love for the Father-land he will put above all personal ambition his nation's welfare and its future greatness." Some 14 years later, in 1934, when the dictator had not only materialised but had also been elected leader of the German

The link between Hess and the Duke of Hamilton was extremely tenuous and not at all as *The Bulletin* reported. Nevertheless, the Duke's house was indeed Hess's destination; the Duke's sympathy was to be enlisted to his cause; Hess was to be conducted as an envoy to King George VI, who would then negotiate peace with the Reich after dismissing from power the aggressive Government of Churchill and other warmongers. Newspaper accounts of Hess's conduct on arrival are consistent with this delusion. Hess apparently saw himself as an honourable ambassador, not as refugee, nor as a spy.

This is how *The Glasgow Herald* of Tuesday, 13th May broke the news:

PARACHUTE LANDING IN DUSK

Hess shows coolness in Ploughman's Cottage

Darkness was falling when Hess made his parachute landing on a Renfrewshire farm on Saturday night.

The crash of his plane was heard over a wide area. People rushed to the spot, but were kept at a safe distance by members of the Home Guard, who little suspected the distinguished nature of their first parachutist haul.

When Hess arrived over the area where he intended to land, his machine was heard circling for some time. Soon afterwards it dived to the ground, falling on a field of the farm. The airman came down on a nearby field, landing almost at the door of the ploughman's cottage. The ploughman, David McLean, rushed to the door and found the airman busily divesting himself of his parachute gear.

When Mr McLean and his mother were visited by *The Glasgow Herald* reporter last night they had just heard the news of the German radio broadcast of the disappearance of Hess. "We were wondering if it was Hess," they said. "There was some excitement in the kitchen when the military people came to take him away, but he was the coolest man of the whole lot." Mr McLean said the German airman had a slight scar on the neck. When he smiled he revealed several gold teeth. The clothing showing below his flying kit was of good quality and according to Mrs McLean he wore boots of fine leather "just like gloves." On one wrist he wore a gold watch and on the other a gold compass. Mr McLean said there was no sign of his suffering from hallucinations such as the German wireless spoke about Hess. "He was perfectly composed though tired. He spoke like any sane man. He gave his age as forty-six."

He was completely unarmed when he baled out — and his plane also carried no bombs, nor had his guns been fired. Petrol was running low and as a landing seemed impossible, he resolved that there was nothing else for it than to bale out and let the plane crash in a field. Seconds after he had jumped by parachute the machine crashed with a roar on a field — killing a young hare. He was rolling on his back on the ground, extricating himself from the parachute gear when Mr McLean suddenly stood over him and said — "Who are you? What are you doing here?" Without showing any signs of fright or anxiety to escape, the airman spoke to him in almost perfect English.

"He was limping badly. His left leg seemed to have got a wrench when he landed," said Mr McLean when recounting the experience. "He was a thorough gentleman. I could tell that from his bearing and by the way he spoke. He sat down in an easy chair by the fireside. My mother got up out of bed, dressed, and came through to the kitchen to see our unusual visitor."

"Will you have a cup of tea?" Mrs McLean asked him. "No," he replied, "I do not drink tea at night, thank you."

He then asked for water and two young soldiers, who had been attracted to the farm by the sound of the plane crashing, jocularly remarked, "It's beer we drink in Britain." Hess replied, "Oh yes, we drink plenty of beer too in Munich where I come from."

The plane, the wreckage of which was strewn around a field not far from the ploughman's cottage, was guarded all day yesterday, and sightseers had to be kept at a distance.

The Messerschmidt was, of course, removed for examination. On the Saturday of that week it was on display in Trafalgar Square at the head of a parade promoted by the National Savings Committee. A week later it was on display in Oxford.

The McLeans and the Home Guardsmen who had spoken to Hess énjoyed another day of limelight as the Press awaited developments from London. Born in Dundee, David McLean had served for three years in the First World War with the King's Own Scottish Borderers and the Royal Scots Fusiliers. After seven years in Australia in farm work he had come as ploughman to the Bairds at Floors, and his mother kept house for him. Jack Paterson and Robert Gibson also found their prisoner perfectly sane, though a little excited. They offered first a cigarette — he didn't smoke — and then, for want of beer, milk, which he did take although apparently he showed some surprise that they even had milk.

What, however, of Rudolf Hess's claim to be on visiting terms with the Duke of Hamilton? 'Captain Horn' had asked his way to Dungavel, a request which was naturally ignored, but in captivity he refused to speak to anyone other than the Duke. The commandant at Maryhill contacted the RAF Sector Controller at Turnhouse, under whose orders the Duke was serving. Hamilton was summoned immediately although it was the early hours of Sunday morning. He was informed that the pilot of the Messerschmidt that had recently crashed in the West of Scotland wished to see him personally — name and rank, Oberleutnant Alfred Horn. The name meant nothing to the Duke.

The encounters which subsequently took place and from which the identification of the prisoner emerged are best presented in the words of the Duke of Hamilton's son, Lord James Douglas-Hamilton, whose book "Motive for a Mission" recounts and analyses the story of this mysterious flight.*

> Hamilton made arrangements with the Intelligence office — whose duty it was to interrogate German pilots — to leave for Glasgow early on the next day. He returned to his house by the airfield and, remembering that he had noted the names of various Luftwaffe officers whom he had met during the Olympic Games in 1936, looked through his list. However, Horn's name did not appear, so Hamilton returned to bed, somewhat puzzled but in readiness for what the next day might hold in store.
>
> On Sunday 11th May 1941 Hamilton, together with the RAF Interrogating Officer, arrived at Maryhill Barracks at 10 a.m.

* Macmillan, 1971, pp. 157 ff.

115

Hamilton first examined the personal effects of the prisoner, which included a Leica camera, a map, a large number of medicines, photographs of the prisoner as a small boy, and the visiting card of General Professor Karl Haushofer and his son, Dr Albrecht Haushofer . . . .

Accompanied by the Interrogating Officer and the Military Officer on guard, Hamilton entered the prisoner's room. . . . . Hamilton had no recollection of having seen him before, and the prisoner immediately asked that Hamilton should speak to him alone. The other officers were requested by Hamilton to withdraw, which they did. The most accurate record of what followed is given in Hamilton's report to the Prime Minister. –

The German opened by saying he had seen me in Berlin at the Olympic Games in 1936 . . . . He said, "I do not know if you recognise me, but I am Rudolf Hess." He went on to say he was on a mission of humanity and that the Fuehrer did not want to defeat England and wished to stop fighting. His friend Albrecht Haushofer told him I was an Englishman who he thought would understand his (Hess's) point of view . . . . he had tried to fly to Dungavel and this was the fourth time he had set out, the first time being in December. On the three previous occasions he had turned back owing to bad weather.

The fact that Reich Minister Hess had come to this country in person would, he stated, show his sincerity and Germany's willingness for peace . . . . Germany would win the war . . . . He wanted to stop the unnecessary slaughter. He asked me if I could get together leading members of my party to talk over things with a view to making peace proposals . . . . He requested me to ask the King to give him 'parole' as he had come unarmed and of his own free will. He further asked me if I could inform his family he was safe by sending a telegram to Rothacker, Hertzogstr. 17, Zurich, (an aunt) stating that Alfred Horn was in good health. He also asked that his identity should not be disclosed to the Press . . . . and "Will you please have me moved out of Glasgow as I am anxious not to be killed by a German bomb?" . . .

I believed that this prisoner was indeed Hess himself.

Hamilton collected some of the photographs of the prisoner and told the Officer Commanding that the prisoner was probably very important, and that a strong guard should be put over him. He drove back to Turnhouse airport in the afternoon. . . . . Having obtained leave from his Air Marshall, he rang up and asked to see Sir Alexander Cadogan, the head of the Foreign Office . . . . unsuccessfully.

In frustration Hamilton immediately telephoned 10 Downing Street and spoke to Jack Colville, the Prime Minister's Private Secretary, demanding to see the Prime Minister and without delay . . . . Hamilton said that something extraordinary had taken place, but declined to reveal what the extraordinary event was. All he did say was that it was like something out of an E. Phillip Oppenheimer novel . . . . Hamilton said he would be at Northolt within two hours and asked Colville to make necessary arrangements. . . .

Hamilton then took off for Northolt in a Hurricane and assembled his thoughts as he flew . . . . When he landed at Northolt he was given a message to fly on to Kidlington, near Oxford. The Prime Minister's car was waiting to take him to Ditchley Park . . . .They were finishing dinner and Churchill welcomed Hamilton with great enthusiasm and asked him for his news. . . . As the room was full of guests Hamilton replied that he must communicate his news to the Prime Minister in private. Accordingly the guests automatically withdrew, leaving the Prime Minister, Hamilton and Sir Archibald Sinclair (the Secretary of State for Air). Hamilton then explained that a German pilot had arrived in Scotland, had given the name of Oberleutnant Alfred Horn to everyone else, and had then told him personally that he was Rudolf Hess.

Hamilton had the impression that Churchill was looking at him sympathetically, as though he were suffering from war strain and hallucinations. . . . . "Do you mean to tell me that the Deputy Fuehrer of Germany is in our hands?" Hamilton replied that the man had certainly declared himself to be Hess. Hamilton then produced the photographs of the unidentified prisoner. Churchill looked at them and said, "Well, Hess or no Hess I am going to see the Marx Brothers."

By the time the film show finished the Prime Minister had decided that it was necessary to go into the matter thoroughly, the time being about midnight. For the next three hours Hamilton went through every detail and was asked every

117

conceivable type of question. . . . . Hamilton also said that Hess, if he was Hess, had said that Mr Churchill would not be very sympathetic to his point of view. After a momentary pause Churchill replied, "By God, I would not!"

Hamilton was sworn to secrecy . . . . Hess's peace overture could not have been made in a more unconventional and unexpected way.

They retired to bed. Next morning Hamilton accompanied Churchill to Downing Street where they were joined by the Foreign Secretary, Anthony Eden. Eden's diary entry for that 'incredible day' May 12th, records seeing the photographs: "I said they appeared to be of Hess. The Prime Minister was much impressed, not having believed the story." (*Memoirs: The Reckoning,* 1964.)

Confirmation of identity was the priority. Hamilton flew back to Scotland that same evening with the German affairs expert from the Foreign Office, Mr Ivone Kirkpatrick. On landing at Turnhouse they heard that the German wireless had just announced that Hess was missing. This dispelled any lingering doubts and by 1 a.m. positive identification that the Deputy Fuehrer was in British hands was confirmed to the Foreign Secretary.

In his *Memoirs,* Sir Anthony Eden concluded his comments on Hess: —

Hess had a sanguine belief in the power of Dukes in Britain . . . . The drama of Hess's escapade never ceased to fascinate the Russians who found it difficult to believe that there was not something sinister behind it; in which the British Government was in some way implicated. Over and over again within the next few years I was cross-examined about it by Molotov . . . . Though I told him all the details and offered to show them the dossier of Hess's statements, I doubt if they were ever really satisfied that the incident was as unexpected and inexplicable to us as to them.

President Roosevelt, despite a long and full report from Mr Churchill, is also on record as having wondered if the British Government was not concealing something.

The link between Albrecht Haushofer, son of Karl Haushofer exponent of the theory of Geopolitik and Lebensraum so dear to the Nazis, and the Duke of Hamilton, is fully explored in "Motive for a Mission". Much of this book portrays the complexities of German political life during the 1920s and 30s as the power of the National Socialist Party steadily increased. A secret letter from Albrecht Haushofer to the Duke of Hamilton had been intercepted by wartime censorship and − unknown to Haushofer and, of course, Hamilton − had encouraged Hess to undertake his hopeless personal mission. Never a party member, Albrecht Haushofer was executed in Berlin shortly before the end of the War for suspected complicity in the plot to overthrow Hitler.

For a second week at the House of Commons' Question Time the Prime Minister chose to fend off questions about Hess's arrival and status. Any lingering anxiety, however, about the role of the Duke of Hamilton was allayed.

Tuesday 20th May:

Question: . . . . has it yet been established whether the projected visit of the Deputy Fuehrer of the Reich to the Duke of Hamilton was planned with the connivance and support of the German Government?

The Prime Minister: I am not yet in a position to make a statement on this subject, and I am not at all sure when I shall be.

Supplementary Question: While I appreciate the necessity for discretion on the part of my right honourable Friend, may I ask him whether the Government has actively in mind the possibility that the whole stunt may be a common or garden plant, and further will my right honourable Friend discourage sections of the Press from any renewal of their nauseating rhapsodies on this blood-stained crook?

The Prime Minister: Certainly I do not feel I ought to detract in any way from the vehemence of the honourable and gallant Member.

Question: . . . . will the Prime Minister take an early opportunity of allaying public anxiety on *one* point in this affair, namely, the statement made in some newspapers that a citizen of this country received a private letter from Hess in Germany?

The Prime Minister: The honourable Member is no doubt referring to the Duke of Hamilton. I have suggested that a Question should be put on the Order Paper for the Third Sitting Day, and it will be answered by the Secretary of State for Air, under whose authority the noble Duke is serving.

Question: . . . . as to the Press, did my right honourable Friend notice that *The Times* described this creature as an idealist?

The Prime Minister: I do not think I can indulge in this retrospective examination of the Press. There has been a great public interest in this man. We were not able to give any guidance, the Germans gave different guidance every day, and the Press naturally endeavoured to satisfy the public desire for information by recalling all kinds of details which came to their hands. It seems to me that the whole episode has been entertaining as well as important.

A remark from his *History of the Second World War* underlines Churchill's appreciation of the sheer curiosity value of the incident. "It was as if my trusted colleague the Foreign Secretary, who was only a little younger than Hess, had parachuted from a stolen Spitfire into the grounds of Berchtesgaden."

On the "Third Sitting Day" in response to a question from Major Guy Lloyd (who in 1940 had succeeded the Duke of Hamilton as M.P. for East Renfrewshire), this statement was made to the House by the Secretary of State for Air:

When Deputy Fuehrer Hess came with his aeroplane to Scotland on May 10, he gave a false name and asked to see the Duke of Hamilton. The Duke, being apprised by the authorities, visited the German prisoner in hospital. Hess then revealed for the first time his true identity, saying that he had seen the Duke when he was at the Olympic Games at Berlin in 1936.

The Duke did not recognise the prisoner and had never met the Deputy Fuehrer. (*Cheers*) He had, however, visited Germany for the Olympic Games in 1936, and during that time had attended more than one large public function at which German ministers were present. It is therefore quite possible that the

Deputy Fuehrer may have seen him on one such occasion. As soon as the interview was over Wing Commander the Duke of Hamilton flew to England and gave a full report of what had passed to the Prime Minister.

Contrary to reports which have appeared in some of the newspapers the Duke has never been in correspondence with the Deputy Fuehrer. (*Cheers*) None of the Duke's three brothers, who are, like himself, serving in the RAF, has either met Hess or had correspondence with him. It will be seen that the conduct of the Duke of Hamilton has been in every respect honourable and proper. (*Cheers*)

Further questions ensued as to what lay behind Hess's flight and such was the dissatisfaction at the Government's silence that an Adjournment Debate was sought. This took place on June 19th with Mr Butler, one of Eden's assistant ministers, as the main speaker for the Government. The proceedings can be read in Volume 372 of Hansard, pp 885–922. The matter was no longer newsworthy, having been overtaken by the march of events.

Churchill's side of the story can be read in *The History of the Second World War*. His account includes the full text of the long, confidential cable he, alias "Former Naval Person", sent on 17th May 1941 to President Roosevelt, which concluded : "Here we think it best to let the Press have a good run for a bit and keep the Germans guessing."

The German propaganda machine took great pains to discredit Hess. In the early hours of 19th May two plain clothes SS men were arrested near Luton, searchlights having detected their descending parachutes. A map in their possession had a circle round Dungavel, Hess's destination when he arrived at Floors Farm. Under the rules of war they were interrogated and executed. Hess had arrived in uniform. Here are the words with which Hess finished the letter he left for Hitler when he flew off from Augsburg that fateful evening: "and if, my Fuehrer, this project . . . . ends in failure . . . . simply say I was crazy."

In only one of his beliefs about British political life had Hess been correct: dukes of the realm do dine with the King. On Friday, 11th June, at Windsor Castle, the Duke of Hamilton was entertained to lunch by King George VI.

Royal Observer Corps plotted track of Me 110, 10-5-41.

22.25   visual identification made by A3 post, Chatton, Northumberland.

23.09   crash landing witnessed by H2 post, Eaglesham Moors, who called up HQ in Glasgow with grid reference and message:

"One man has just baled out and looks like landing safely. Plane has come down out of control and crashed in flames."

HQ immediately alerted Home Guard and local police.

OPEN~AIR HOSPITAL ....
at SOUTHFIELD

The afternoon of Sunday 3rd July 1949 found the Kirkintilloch Junior Choir and Springburn Military Band in the grounds of Mearnskirk Hospital. The occasion was to celebrate the unveiling of a bronze statue of Peter Pan — a memorial to the hospital's first Physician Superintendent, Dr John A. Wilson, O.B.E.

Following War service and laboratory research work in bacteriology, Dr Wilson joined the Tuberculosis Service of Glasgow Corporation, working in the East End and at Ruchill Hospital, until in 1929 he became Superintendent of Mearnskirk Hospital for Children, then still under construction. At the same time he became Senior Lecturer in Clinical Tuberculosis at Glasgow University. Both posts he held with distinction until his death in July, 1946.

Why Peter Pan? During the 1930s Dr Wilson, who was always keenly concerned to enhance the beauty of the extensive grounds and to delight the many child patients, had arranged for the erection of several small statues of child figures. They were made of cement and thus vulnerable to the elements in so exposed a position as Mearnskirk. Dr Wilson, therefore, wished for a bronze statue which would last — and, in particular, a representation of J.M. Barrie's 'eternal child', Peter Pan. Perhaps the doctor's interest in Barrie's Peter stemmed partly from the fact that his father-in-law had been one of Barrie's boyhood friends in Kirriemuir. The copyright of the play and story had been donated by Barrie to Great Ormonde Street Sick Children's Hospital in London. "Peter" is, however, also part of the Mearnskirk scene.

The coming of War delayed any realisation of Dr Wilson's plans, but afterwards during his final illness he was promised by his friend Mr Alfred Ellsworth that "Peter" would soon come to Mearnskirk. This promise led to a Peter Pan/Dr Wilson Memorial Fund being launched and its fulfilment came with the unveiling ceremony in the summer of 1949. A souvenir brochure marked the occasion, in which Alex Proudfoot R.S.A., the sculptor, described his commission and the genesis of the bronze Peter Pan.

In January 1948, my telephone rang and when I lifted the receiver a voice asked, "Are you Proudfoot the Sculptor?" "I am," I replied. "Can you make a Peter Pan?" the voice went on. "Yes," I said, "I can try at least." The voice was that of Mr Alfred Ellsworth and I heard from him of his promise to the late Dr Wilson to provide a "Peter Pan" embodying the story of Barrie's fanciful creation, to be placed in a suitable site somewhere in the grounds of Mearnskirk Hospital.

I was delighted to accept the commission and on deciding to proceed, my first approach to the job was to read all about Peter Pan again and so get into the full spirit of the adventure. The great imaginative fact about Peter was that he could fly and that children who believed in him could also fly; they could soar about in the world of imagination just like him. So I sketched a model in clay showing him as if he were sailing through the air and blowing his trumpet to call all children.

Now you cannot have a bronze figure, even of Peter, hanging in the air without something to support it, so I had to put Peter's right foot on the back of a tortoise and his left foot on the nose of a rabbit which is just poking its head up out of a hole, and all this had to be placed on a pedestal.

Then something of the story of Peter had to be told; so four panels were designed to go round the pedestal. The first shows some of the pirates with Smee and Captain Hook in the middle and Cecco the Italian listening with his ear to the ground, Indian fashion. The second shows the children, Wendy, Michael and John, flying after Peter to the Never-Never-Land, Tinker Bell, with her light, leading the way. On the beach in the foreground the crocodile lies in wait for Captain Hook and mermaids sun themselves. In the distance to the right appear the wigwams of the Indians. The third panel shows the animals from the jungle, a lion leading the way. They are chasing the Indians and a pair of rabbits are pushing the lion forward. Peter is seated on the back of a kangaroo which is making a flying leap over the elephant who is throwing a shower of water from his trunk towards the Indians. Two wolves and a pair of monkeys are also seen and two imps of mischief. The fourth panel shows the Indians in Indian file. They are in their war-paint and with their various weapons are hot on the trail of the Pirates; at the same time they keep a watch at the rear for the animals of the jungle.

125

So we have the animals chasing the Indians and the Indians chasing the Pirates and the Pirates chasing Peter, all according to the story.

When the design was approved the next step was to enlarge the work to the full size. . . . . The enlarging was done in clay and when completed was moulded and cast in plaster by Mr George Mancini who also cast the complete figure in bronze. The casting of this figure, owing to its action and its slight contact with the base, presented several difficulties to the founder, but they were all successfully overcome and so we have our "Peter Pan", Barrie's immortality boy, soaring along airily, just as we hope Dr Wilson would have liked to have seen him, had he lived to see his wish realised.

That is the story of the coming of Peter Pan to Mearnskirk: a fitting memorial to the first superintendent and a lovely statue for lovely grounds.

Originally the estate policies of Southfield House, the grounds had deteriorated during changes of tenancy at the turn of the century. Happily the opening of the Children's Hospital led to

their restoration. In 1913 the Corporation of Glasgow bought Southfield House and its policies, along with the farms of Hazelden Head, Westfield, Eastfield and Langrig. Their original intention had been to convert the mansion-house into a country home for pre-tuberculous children. Building operations were delayed by the 1914—18 War, during which the mansionhouse deteriorated to such an extent that it had to be demolished. The present rock-gardens and walls incorporate many of its stones. Pavilions were planned to treat 160 adults and 300 children suffering from TB. The name of the institution was to be Southfield Sanatorium, but this was discarded because of the Edinburgh hospital of the same name. The name 'Mearnskirk' was adopted in deference to the proximity of Mearns Parish Kirk, and having dropped the plan to have adult beds, the full name became 'Mearnskirk Hospital for Children'.

Building began in 1921, Dr Wilson became superintendent in 1929, and the first patients were received in 1930. Dr Dale, then assistant to Dr Wilson and his successor as superintendent, described the opening days thus:

On the 1st of May 1930 the sun shone brightly as Medical, Nursing, Domestic and other staff, sufficient to run Pavilions 1, 2 and 3, began to arrive. The newcomers quickly settled into their quarters and work began. All were anxious to see the kitchen staff on friendly terms with their equipment and were relieved to note that everything was in working order. Lunch may have been a trifle sketchy that day but it was on the table punctually at 1 p.m. The final issue of equipment proceeded and the nurses busied themselves with linen marking and the hundred and one jobs which form a necessary preliminary to the admission of patients.

The first patients arrived as arranged on 9th May and were children suffering from surgical tuberculosis, transferred from Robroyston Hospital where they had been accommodated pending the opening of Mearnskirk. The first patient was George McEwan, aged 6 years, who stepped from the ambulance proudly carrying a large box of cigarettes for Dr Wilson from the staff at Robroyston. That was, of course, in 1930 when cigarettes could be had at any tobacconist at a mere shilling for twenty.

Later in the year Pavilions 4, 5 and 6 were opened and by

the Spring of 1931 Pavilions 7, 8 and 9 were completed and occupied.

The hospital was officially opened by H.R.H. the Duchess of York (now the Queen Mother) on 12th October 1932. To mark the occasion Her Royal Highness planted a royal oak on the main avenue and this tree has grown and flourished with the development of the hospital.

Pre-war Mearnskirk with its broad verandahs was primarily a children's orthopaedic hospital, treating children with TB of the spine, hip and other bones and joints. As treatment was often prolonged, the educational, recreational and spiritual needs of the young patients had also to be addressed. Teachers were employed and hosts of friends visited, ran Scouts, Guides, Sunday Schools, and so on. Dr Wilson's recognition of the importance of these activities for his patients' wellbeing was not outweighed by his clinical interests in pulmonary TB or his bacteriological research work. The staff were similarly minded. Perhaps the relative isolation and the beautiful surroundings contributed to

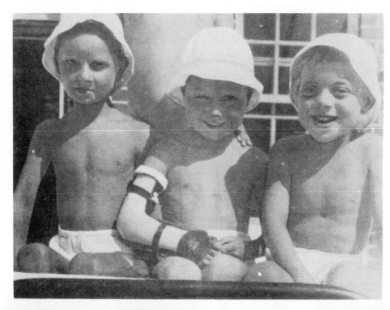

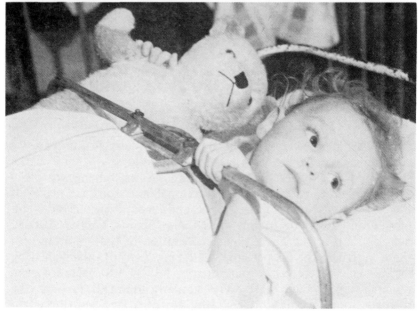

129

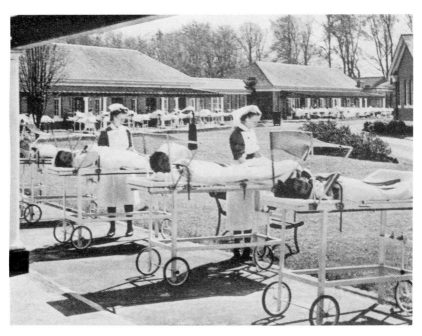

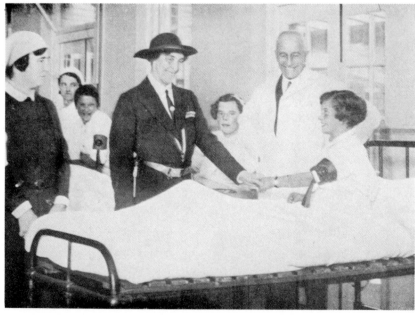

this very special quality of Mearnskirk care which Dr Dale later defined as "the spirit of Mearnskirk".

Among the many regular visitors and loyal friends of the hospital from its earliest days, none is better known than the Rev. W. Murray Mackay, who in 1985 retired after over fifty years of chaplaincy duties. Mr Mackay recalls walking through a ward with Dr Dale – as he did many a time, Dr Dale being an elder in Newton Mearns Church – and Dr Dale saying: "Mr Mackay, I believe that the Church should always be *seen* in a hospital: that is indeed the heart of the matter." In 1933 Mr Mackay and Mr James Rodger of the Christian Brethren led thirty helpers in Sunday School work among the children. This resumed after the War but, as the proportion of adults to children changed, Sunday School meetings were replaced by short Praise Services. When Mr Rodger died in 1975 his Sunday by Sunday service to Mearnskirk Hospital spanned over forty years and he had been joined by hundreds of helpers from many Southside meetings and churches. Under the leadership of Mr Alex Muirhead of Victoria Hall, and later Mr Jack Fraser of Stamperland, seventy or eighty 'Sunday Singers' continue to bring favourite hymns and God's Word to the wards each Sunday morning.

Sunday is no different from weekdays so far as friends of Mearnskirk are concerned. Individuals and groups vie with each other in the generous giving of their time. An example is the following tribute which appeared in *The Glasgow Herald* in January 1980.

HOSPITAL MOURNS FOR 'MRS THURSDAY'

'Mrs Thursday', who faithfully visited hospital patients on Thursdays for 30 years, has died aged 83. Mrs Jane Moore of Fordyce Court, Newton Mearns, continued the visits until three years ago when she became blind. Her interests in the welfare of patients at Mearnskirk Hospital, Newton Mearns, never waned. At Christmas she sent them a best wishes telegram.

Two years ago hospital staff wanted to nominate her as Scotswoman of the Year, but she declined to enter.

Mrs Emily Aird, senior nursing officer at Mearnskirk, said last night: "I came here 25 years ago and Mrs Thursday was an institution even then. She provided gifts of sweets and magazines out of her own pocket although a pensioner, and even when her eyesight deteriorated she continued to visit by taxi."

Mrs Ishbel Woods, a retired sister at Mearnskirk said: "We understand Mrs Moore started the visits after seeing a friend in the hospital and realising that many of the patients rarely received visitors."

Much has of course changed at Mearnskirk since its days as a Corporation of Glasgow children's TB sanatorium. Improved living conditions and the development of drug treatments have almost eradicated the disease. Nevertheless, the "spirit of Mearnskirk" remains. Nowadays most patients are again long stay as the hospital plays a major role in geriatric care for the south side of Glasgow.

In 1948 with the inception of the National Health Service, the hospital transferred from the control of the Corporation of Glasgow to the Western Regional Hospital Board and the Board of Management for the Glasgow Victoria Hospitals. Later that year an Ear, Nose and Throat Department was established, which was active until 1986. Thus children with tonsilitis and similar complaints came to Mearnskirk, fortunately measuring their stay in days rather than the months or years of the children before the War. Since 1959 Mearnskirk has been officially designated a General Hospital; different treatment and services have been offered as medical and political priorities have changed.

At the outbreak of World War II in a hospital of 500 beds over 4,000 children and 300 adults had received treatment. The Emergency Medical Service took over most of the pavilions during the war years, 287 children having been evacuated to Millport. A hutted Annexe was built to add 600 beds and the E.M.S. provided treatment for more than 33,000 naval personnel. After the War the allocation of 582 beds was balanced slightly towards children, but since the later fifties the emphasis has shifted steadily in favour of adults, especially the elderly.

Following the release of the hospital from Emergency Service on 31st August 1946, and as a direct result of innovations in the surgical treatment of pulmonary TB, Pavilion 7 was converted into a fully equipped theatre unit capable of dealing with all aspects of Thoracic Surgery. The first patients were admitted in November 1946. Mr Bruce Dick of Hairmyres Hospital was visiting consultant surgeon and in charge of the day to day running of the unit was Mr R.S. Barclay. Under their leadership a highly skilled specialist medical, scientific, and nursing team was built up, and Mearnskirk became recognised as a leading centre for heart and lung surgery, renowned both in Britain and abroad.

Members of the team travelled extensively to exchange views on techniques. Mr Barclay, for example, recalls visits to European centres at Leyden, Munich, Paris and further afield to Houston, Texas and San Francisco. From 1951 to 1956 extra patient beds were used in Davos and Leysin, Switzerland, and five times each year visits were made to see which patients might benefit from coming 'home' to Mearnskirk for operations. In the heyday of the team's operative work at Mearnskirk they too were much visited from overseas: in November 1958, for instance, Soviet visitors under the auspices of the Scottish Soviet Friendship Society were entertained. With the advent of streptomycin, however, most TB patients recovered without recourse to major chest surgery.

Babies born with 'a hole in the heart' also came to Mearnskirk for operative treatment. By lowering the temperature from 37°C (normal) to 30°C, it was possible for the brain to withstand a lack of oxygen for up to seven minutes, during which time uncomplicated holes could be closed. Adult operations included opening the mitral valve (which had perhaps closed as a result of rheumatic fever). The introduction of the Heart/Lung Machine allowed the operational time to be extended to hours; thus more complicated lesions could be treated, valves replaced, and so on. When visiting Houston Mr Barclay witnessed one of the world's first heart transplant operations.

As part of a reorganisation of specialist care in Glasgow hospitals and to the regret of the team, this unit was closed in the mid-seventies. Staff either retired or dispersed. The work was, of course, changing. Chemotherapy and mass radiography campaigns eliminated the need for surgery in TB cases. The emphasis had shifted from thoracic to cardiac operations and further N.H.S. developments were centralised in the longer established heart units of the Western, Royal, and Sick Children's Hospitals.

135

The retirement of Mr Kenneth Guest in 1977 from the position of consultant orthopaedic surgeon brought another chapter in Mearnskirk history to a close. The position was not renewed and orthopaedic patients now come to Mearnskirk only to convalesce from operations which have already been performed at the Victoria Infirmary.

Treatments change, staff and patients come and go, but day by day, month by month, year by year, the work of healing and caring continues in each of the red and white 'butterfly' pavilions with their glass-roofed, southwest-facing verandahs, surrounded by lawns, flower borders and majestic trees. North of the main avenue lies the Princess Elizabeth Playground, which the present Queen gifted to Mearnskirk's children on the occasion of her marriage to Prince Philip. On the eastern part of this extensive grassy area a new pavilion, specially designed for old people, has been built. Adjacent, a 'therapy' garden has been landscaped. In the words of the nursing staff introducing their Golden Jubilee Pictorial Album in 1980: "Whatever the next half-century holds for Mearnskirk, there is no doubt that it will remain a hospital that is adaptable and ever ready to serve."

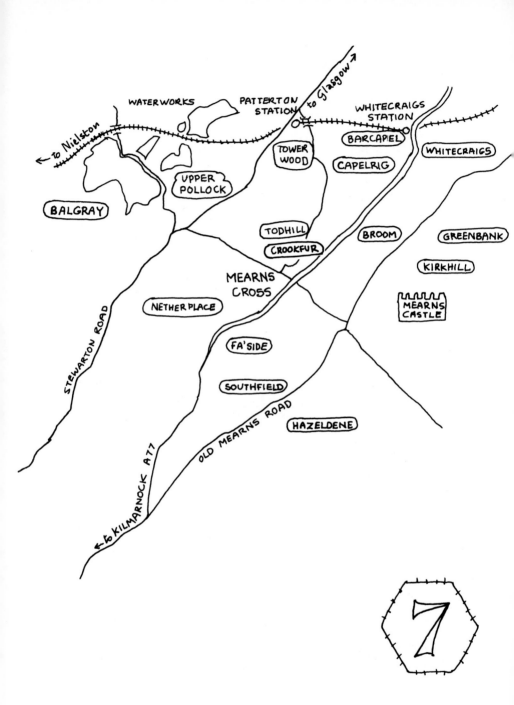

BIG HOUSES......
no more

The beautiful wooded grounds of Mearnskirk Hospital are a reminder of the many fine estates of earlier times. Forty-seven heritors with the valuation of their properties were listed in the Second Statistical Account. They ranged from Mr Harvie of Greenlaw at £8 to the Polloks of Upper Pollok at £1,409.5.10, and totalled £4,725.6.6 (Scots). The higher valuations were Hazelden £212, and Southfield £205, Capelrig £182, Greenbank £165, Watten £137, Middleton £131, and Blackhouse £97. Further two figure amounts included such familiar names as Shaw, Fingleton, Burnhouse, Broom, Townhead, Maidenhill, Duncarnock, Malletsheugh, Kirkhill, Titwood, Flook, Cairn, Walton, Crook, Faside, Roadenhead, and Humbie. The Rev. MacKellar expressed admiration for the "excellent modern mansions" of his country parish.

Although most of these properties survived into the 20th century, few remain nowadays in anything like their original form. Gone, for example, is the property which headed Mr MacKellar's valuation list – POLLOK CASTLE. In 1703 the laird of Upper Pollok was knighted – Sir Robert Pollok of Pollok. The family

Pollok Castle, Mearns.

was a branch of the Maxwell/Pollok family of Nether Pollok (now Pollok Park of Glasgow). Several houses have graced the estate; the last one (dating from 1886) was built in the "Scots baronial" style by the Fergusson Polloks, last of the line. Like its predecessor, this splendid mansion was severely damaged by fire and ultimately had to be demolished. The wooded estate remains, carpeted every spring with bluebells and daffodils. The former lodge houses and stables have been converted into private houses. In Mearns Parish Kirk the oak pulpit carved with a Celtic cross bears the crest of the Polloks. It was gifted to the church in memory of the Pollok family by its last surviving member, Miss Fergusson Pollok.

At the heart of present-day Newton Mearns lies Crookfur Estate — now the Crookfur Cottage Homes. Until the 1950s CROOKFUR was the home of the Templetons, a branch of the carpet manufacturing family of Glasgow's "Doge Palace" fame. A vivid picture of Crookfur grounds and glasshouses was given to readers of the Horticultural Society Centenary Year Book by Alan MacCallum, gardener to the Templeton family between the wars:

Crookfur House . . . . was a charming old Mansion clad in front with ivy, the windows looked out on to a pleasant lawn and the planted grounds around, studded with hardy trees among which were fine groups of rhododendron. Shady walks pursued a wandering course around the grounds and were enjoyable retreats even for the gardeners in hot summer days. Countless snowdrops and daffodils were naturalised in clusters and drifts and were a delight in the grass around the bare feet of the trees in spring.

Flower beds at the front of the house were avoided due to the depredations of rabbits. Attempts to naturalise croci had been given up for the same reason. However, the flower garden, which was within the main walled garden, was within easy reach of the front door. The walled garden was probably an acre in extent; a gravel path edged with boxwood ran round the garden with ribbon borders up to the walls, on which apples and plums were trained. There were also two small orchards; one which had a north-east exposure returned little, but I believe no other crop would have succeeded better.

Grass walks intersected the rose and flower beds and were mown with an eighteen inch tracing mower, myself pulling in front and another man pushing at the back. The main lawn was cut with a thirty-six inch horse-drawn mower which must have weighed fully three hundredweight. The motive power, a fresh hunter, had to be tethered to a stake in the field and trotted around for a couple of hours before being yoked. Grass Mowing Day was an exciting if exhausting business with this animal. I was much relieved when the decision was taken to hire a 'staid, canny' Clydesdale for this job. In a few years, however, we had a petrol-driven machine and could mow the lawns when convenient for us rather than the hiring contractor.

The roses were old: a large bed of the damask rose known as York and Lancaster thrived as did the moss roses, the only one of which I recall being Crimson Globe. Hybrid perpetuals included Mrs John Laing, Hugh Dickson and Frau Karl Drushki; and hybrid teas Mme Caroline Testout, Mme Abel Chatenay and Mme Ravery.

Crysanths too were featured and like the roses were the old-fashioned spray varieties – White Masse, Mme Marie Masse, Horace Martin, Pollie and Coacher's Crimson. The names of these varieties will bring back memories to older gardeners. In the twenties a new race of early flowering Japanese chrysanths were being bred; the first I grew was Bronze Early Buttercup, the parent of many of today's handsome large well-formed varieties. It was the same with dahlias – at that time flower formation and colour was quite good, but the stems were so weak they were unable to support the head in an upright position. Antirrhinums, asters, stocks and nemesia were all used extensively . . . .

The glass consisted of a peach house, a vinery, a fig house, and a fernery. Two greenhouses stood apart from the main range. One had been a melon house prior to a fault in the heating system, and thereafter housed camellias in winter and spring, growing tomatoes when the camellias were put out for the summer once flowering was past. The other was used for the cultivation of pelargoniums both regal and zonal. I can remember the 'geraniums' on the wall of the peach house – King of Denmark and Barbara Hope, fully ten feet tall. There were always some flowers showing, even in winter, and from April till June hundreds of large trusses could be gathered. Peaches when established are very large croppers and when properly cultivated give excellent results. Royal George was the variety we grew; a large yellow fruit, mottled and flushed red, with an excellent flavour.

The vines grown here were Black Hamburg, a well-flavoured variety. They were grown as single rods five feet apart and at no time did I ever consider that glass-house vines justified the labour, care and attention that had to be lavished upon them. During the winter manure had to be incorporated into the border, exercising great care to prevent damage to the roots; loose flaky bark had to be removed from the rods, care being taken not to injure the cambium layer; laterals had to be spurred back to two buds of

141

the main rods . . . . rods had to be lowered from training wires in late January and temperatures raised to 55°F at night; syringing was carried out twice daily with tepid water to keep the atmosphere moist. When growth started, rods had to be re-tied; then growth had to be thinned and stopped during spring and summer. Ventilation and temperature needed constant attention. Thinning of bunches required two man days per fortnight from the time of forming to the time of completed growth — a back and neck straining operation standing on a step-ladder with scissors and forked stick. Lovely juicy bunches of grapes resulted with a fine bloom, weighing up to two pounds. In these cost-conscious days, however, fifty shillings a pound would scarcely defray the expense of production. (1969.)

Figs were of easy culture and two crops could be taken, one from the shoots of the previous year's growth and those of the current year for the second crop. The variety grown was Brown Turkey.

The field where the "fresh hunter" had to be trotted before Mr MacCallum could yoke him to the mowing machine lies along-side Ayr Road and nowadays is Crookfur Park. Before the War it was leased for grazing to the Harvies of Shieldhill and Langbank Farms. Their cows had to be chased out of the way whenever "young Mr Templeton" wanted to land his light aeroplane. The story is told that shortly before his marriage he took the staff for a short flight around the district — one at a time — finishing with the housemaids and last of all, the cook. The plane was started by a flick of the propellor and so, having installed the cook, this the son of the house proceeded to do — forgetting he had left the throttle open. Knocking him aside, off went the cook on her first

and last 'solo' flight, the plane careering across the field before coming to rest in a hedge. All parties escaped unscathed apart from decidedly frayed nerves. Perhaps it is fitting that a field of such sporting endeavour now provides facilities for recreations as diverse as football and tap-dancing.

In the 1950s the house was sold and functioned briefly as a Country House Hotel. In the course of changing hands again, the house was so damaged by fire that it had to be demolished. Drapers' trade benevolent organisations acquired the estate in 1960 and seven years later the present Cottage Homes were opened by Lady Fraser of Allander. Designed by Sir Basil Spence, fifty cottages and several groups of self-contained flats have been landscaped into the well-wooded 13 acre estate. A central building, appropriately called Crookfur House, comprises a nursing home, bed-sitting rooms, lounges, dining-room, television room, and the Fraser Hall for concerts and social gatherings. Crookfur Cottage Homes are the third foundation — and the first in Scotland — of the drapery charitable groups known as Cottage Homes and the Scottish Retail Drapers' Benevolent Fund. The residents have two things in common: a working life in the drapery trade and confidence that their retirement years are secure, free from any anxiety about meeting bills or arranging nursing care. Accommodation is rent and rates free although a small contribution is paid by those who can afford it and independent housekeeping is encouraged as long as ability permits. The Homes are in the charge of a Matron. It is claimed that soon after moving in, many of the residents seem years younger and that the expectation of life in the Cottage Homes is several years longer than the national average. Visiting Crookfur this claim is easy to believe; the Cottage Homes do indeed offer their residents an extension of life which is well worth living.

The neighbouring mansion house and estate of THE BROOM did not remain a family home as long as Crookfur. The estate name survives as a district of Mearns; but the mansion house has long had a new name and function — Belmont House School. In 1989 this independent school for boys celebrates its Diamond Jubilee, 56 years of history being at its present site in Broom Estate. This area of Mearns has undergone immense change since Belmont's founder bought the mansion house and two acres of garden, along with a three acre plot for playing fields a short distance away. Broom House could then be approached from two lodge houses on the Kilmarnock (now Ayr) Road. Its main driveway is now Sandringham Avenue, and the stable buildings at the former 'side' entry have recently been redesigned as Lochbroom Court luxury flats. The 'swan pond' remains.

144

In September 1929 G.A. Montague Dale and his wife Beryl opened a preparatory school for boys in Greenhill Avenue near Eastwood Toll, its name BELMONT being an amalgam of their Christian names, Beryl and Montague. The school had grown quickly from its initial roll of 22 and new accommodation was required. The Broom mansion house dates from 1840. The principal rooms on the ground floor were converted into classrooms; the first floor was a mixture of classrooms and dormitories; staff lived on the top floor. North of the Victorian mansion a wooden assembly hall from the Giffnock site was re-erected along with several classrooms and both school and playing fields were surrounded by a high wooden fence. At that time, of course, no houses enclosed the school. This soon changed as Mactaggart and Mickel had bought the estate and began to build houses there before the War. The proximity of Belmont House School was mutually advantageous. Boys were prepared for the Common Entrance Examination, taken at age 13. Few years went by without Belmont House pupils winning Scholarships and Exhibitions to schools such as Fettes and Strathallan. For Belmont's Golden Jubilee in 1979 former pupil Neil Gow, now a Q.C., wrote a short history, enlivened by personal reminiscences, the following excerpts from which characterise the school and its surroundings in the thirties and during the War:

> In the lower forms the school fee was 8 guineas per term, rising to 12 guineas in the higher forms. Extras were offered at 2 guineas per term including pianoforte, elocution, dancing, and boxing; and carpentry lessons could be taken for the cost of the wood used. Haircuts were available once a week for 1/-.
>
> The principal school outfitters were Messrs Rowan of 70 Buchanan Street, Glasgow (now Austin Reeds). The school clothing requirements were extensive and comprehensive, and rigid adherence to the clothing was expected. During the War it was permitted to wear approved cotton dungarees over school clothing to avoid wear and tear. These dungarees proved popular with the boys because, when worn with the school blazer on top, they were the nearest representation of long trousers that most of us could achieve at that age. But no school bag or satchel was required. It was one of the Headmaster's fundamental principles

145

that there should be no homework, and that all preparation should be done at school.

Gerald Arnold Montague Dale, the school's Founder and first Headmaster, came from an Anglican clergy family background. His father was a Canon, and his brother was Assistant Bishop of Guildford and Bishop of Jamaica. Mr Dale — the very mention of that name still recalls feelings of awe and respect in middle-aged Old Boys — was a Prep. School Headmaster of the classical mould. He determined that the school should be run with strong respect for moral principles in a Christian background. He determined to produce "boys of character" rather than great academic scholars although the school has, in fact, always maintained a distinguished record of Scholarships. There was great emphasis on honesty and decency, and 'owning up' when necessary. As a Headmaster he was full of energy and enthusiasm, but beneath his awesome exterior there was real sympathy and kindness, particularly for the boy who tried hard but did not do so well.

His approach is clearly outlined in an Editorial in *The Belmontian* in 1937, which also incidentally emphasises social circumstances and attitudes of the time.

"What is important to realise," he wrote, *"is that living in a big house, having domestic servants, owning a motor car, going to a different school, wearing expensive clothes, are no signs of superiority, and as far as you are concerned, are mere matters of chance. There is no real distinction between the poorest boys in Glasgow, royal princes, and yourselves, and whenever you meet any of them, remember this. It is what you think and say and do — in fact what you are — that makes the difference."*

Nearly all the pupils in the Thirties came from well-to-do families, although perhaps we did not realise it at the time. Most boys attended school from private residences on the south side of Glasgow, particularly Whitecraigs, the Broom Estate as it expanded, Giffnock, Newton Mearns, Clarkston and also Pollokshields. Most houses in those districts which were built in the Twenties and Thirties had a maid's room or servants' quarters attached to the kitchen premises. Some of them had double garages with a flat above for the chauffeur or gardener. When one visited the home of a school friend there was invariably at least

146

a housemaid, and sometimes one or more other domestic servants. All these resident domestics went off to the War, and were never seen again. Presumably they either got married or found something better to do.

In the Thirties, quite a number of boys arrived at Belmont in limousines driven by liveried chauffeurs. However, it must be admitted, sometimes boys from more than one family were carried, although this must have been for reasons of convenience rather than economy. Many boys also had nannies, who arrived at school wearing their long grey coats, black hats and gloves in order to collect their precious charges. Nannies were allowed in the First Form cloakroom only by order of Miss Jackson personally. In Form Two and thereafter, you were expected to tie

your own shoelaces. Those of us who did not actually have nannies were extremely scornful of those who had. At the same time, we were secretly quite glad that our mothers had thought-fully provided us with button-up shoes, instead of those with complicated laces.

Parents of Belmont boys in the Thirties appeared to indulge in a continuous whirl of social activities. As a small boy one was occasionally allowed a brief appearance on evening occasions at home. Everyone arrived in evening dress, usually in groups of four, thus to be conveniently accommodated in the drawing room at the bridge tables covered in plush plum velvet, and provided with score cards and square-barrelled pencils with coloured tassels.

147

The most popular form of entertainment on such occasions was 'sliding', which simply involved running and sliding up and down the ballroom floor until either one's shoes or one's enthusiasm gave out. Half-hearted attempts to initiate "The Grand Old Duke of York" and other children's games were coldly received. The best parties of all were those where, due to lack of adequate supervision, we were allowed to spend most of the afternoon fighting. This would perhaps have been all right if we were wearing tee shirts and jeans, but in those days the standard dress was kilt, sporran and buckled shoes with a silk shirt, and preferably a lace jabot. Such outfits did not commonly survive more than one or two of even the best controlled parties.

The social scene extended even to our level, and it was de rigueur to give a party in a boy's first or second year at school. If the date happened to coincide with a birthday, this was a fact which, for some strange reason, one was absolutely forbidden to disclose.

The most popular venue for such children's parties was the Marlborough House in Shawlands, or the ballroom of the Tudor Cinema* in Giffnock. Parties held in private houses were less popular with parents, because of the substantial risk of destruction to property and furnishings, but were much more popular with the boys, due to the better quality and larger quantities of food provided at home by one's friend's mother.

* Now PRESTO supermarket.

148

Some mothers were actually imprudent enough to ask girls to the party. . . . To invite girls to one's party was complete social disaster, because to some extent it inhibited one's friends from their favourite pursuits of sliding and fighting. Towards the end of such parties we were supposed to sit on the floor and listen to the efforts of a person laughingly described as 'The Entertainer'. Apart from providing the piano accompaniment to "The Grand Old Duke of York", he was supposed to perform a number of tired old conjuring tricks which even six-year-old school boys could see through. When he ran out of ideas he would institute a game of forfeits or would call on us to perform Recitations, both of which were tiresome and embarrassing experiences. The alternative to the entertainer was a silent film show, which in the Thirties was quite exciting. The repertoire of films was usually limited to 'Charlie Chaplin at the Ice Rink', 'Charlie Chaplin and the Fire Brigade', or 'Laurel and Hardy Go a-Haunting'.

Sledging and skating were favourite winter pastimes. After several days of hard frost, skating was possible both on Rouken Glen pond and the Broom pond. Rouken Glen was known to be deeper than Broom pond, but was generally regarded by parents as safer because there was a park ranger who made a vague effort at supervision. If the Broom pond froze over, it was important to see that there was sufficient ice broken to allow the pair of swans to survive.

Each house was allowed to choose periodicals to be supplied for the house room, and a small subscription of 9d was taken for this. In 1937 my house voted for the *Illustrated London News, The Sphere, The Boys' Own Paper, Meccano Magazine, Punch,* and for those who, like myself, could barely read, there was *Chicks Own.*

The school extras were not particularly well supported. Three or four boys took music lessons, but I can only remember one boy who took elocution. Dancing was generally regarded as rather 'cissy' but boxing was more popular. Each Friday afternoon Mr Carswell would come out from his gymnasium in Glasgow to teach us the rudiments of the Noble Art. We spent many happy afternoons in a line, reaching forward simultaneously with our left fist and leg in a passable imitation of a straight left, and right hooks were also very popular. Actual fighting between boys

149

was not permitted until the very end of the lesson, when we were allowed one sixty-second round with a friend of equal size and weight, thus ensuring the rapid and immediate exhaustion of all the participants. In the summer of 1935 the Chief Constable of Glasgow, later to become Sir Percy Sillitoe and Head of Scotland Yard, came out to the school to judge the boxing competition and present the prizes.

One of the most popular activities in the lowest forms was participation in Miss Jackson's Percussion Band. In 1938 the school invested in a complete outfit for her percussion band, including triangles, castanets, tambours, cymbals and drums. We accompanied Miss Jackson's piano playing with a cacophony of sound. The musical notation was written on large sheets measuring about four feet by three feet, pinned to the wall of the classroom. Separate colours of notes indicated which instruments were to play – thus red for triangles, green for castanets, and so on. The cymbals could only be played on the black notes, which appeared very infrequently in the notation, usually at the very end of the tune. Impatient cymbalists occasionally chimed in half way through the tune, much to the general indignation. It is very doubtful whether participation in the percussion band did anything to improve our musical skills or appreciation. My own performance was so poor that the instruments were eventually withdrawn from me and I was relegated to being the conductor.

The award of form medals was introduced at Belmont in the Junior School in 1937. The boy with the best results was allowed to wear the medal on his blazer for the following week. . . . . After the outbreak of War, medals were unobtainable and were not thereafter awarded.

An excitement occurred when a single-decker Western S.M.T. Bus careered off the Kilmarnock Road down an embankment opposite Whitecraigs Golf Club and the driver was killed. Douglas Thomson told us later that after the police had extricated the body of the driver, they had found his boot with his toes still in it. This gruesome and possibly fanciful tale terrified us and for weeks we were afraid to go near the spot.

In the Thirties national events were received with great importance at Belmont. For the Coronation of King George VI in 1937 the school was given five days' holiday. A special commemorative ode was published in *The Belmontian*. A few boys managed to get to London to see the Coronation. Those of us who stayed at home had to be content with hanging Union Jacks out of the front windows. In those days we were very proud of the pre-eminence of Great Britain and the British Empire. We were well aware that one-sixth of the world's population was under British Rule, that the sun never set on the British Empire, and that all the bits coloured pink on the map which hung in Mrs Carswell's classroom in Form Three belonged to us. The Empire Exhibition, held in Bellahouston Park, Glasgow in 1938, was a great attraction and was frequently visited by boys. Empire Day was celebrated on May 25th 1938 and the school was given a whole holiday. Each boy received a certificate with his name on it, stating that he was a citizen of the British Empire, or something of that sort. These certificates were presented by the *Daily Express* on behalf of Lord Beaverbrook, who was at that time promoting a pro-Empire campaign.

The summer of 1939 was hot and long, and even the youngest boys were aware of the dark shadows cast by political events in Europe. . . . . On the morning of 3rd September 1939 my mother, my sister, the housemaid and I solemnly gathered in the drawing room at 11.15 a.m. to hear Mr Chamberlain say on the radio that Herr Hitler had not replied to the British Ultimatum (a new word to me) and therefore "we were at war with Germany." We all stood up to attention as the National Anthem was played. My father's family business of Oil Merchants had been taken over by the Government from September 1st "for the duration" and henceforth all petrol and oil was sold and distributed as "pool petrol".

The school took up the winter term a few days later, and the prospect of War was very exciting for school boys. Immediate developments were the issue of gas masks and the arrival of the evacuees. In the early weeks of September 1939 large numbers of children were evacuated from the Gorbals and Clydeside to the outer suburbs. I remember a clutch of children being shepherded along our road by kindly WVS ladies and being dropped off at various houses in ones and twos. Most of these children did not remain with us more than a week or two before returning home-sick to the City centre. They were as unhappy to be with us as we were to have them. Thus we learned our early lessons in the social inequalities of life.

The Government had arranged for the manufacture of some 34 million gas masks and the issue of the gas masks was clear proof that the War was really on. . . . . Air raid practices were held at school, and when the siren sounded each boy went to his cloak-room peg in the basement corridors, while Mr Dale swooped imperiously up and down the corridors to check that all the staff were on station and no boys were missing. We sat throbbing with excitement, half hoping and expecting at any minute to hear the rattle of canisters of German mustard gas bouncing off the school roof. . . . .

Mobilisation of the armed forces seemed to take quite a long time, but eventually about half of the boys' fathers went off on war service. I cannot remember of any boy's father being killed in action, although this may have happened, but it was not long before the sad news came through of Old Boys who were posted killed or missing in action.

Those fathers who did not serve in the Armed Forces joined the ARP or the LDF, which later became the Home Guard. We used to follow the Home Guard keenly with toy rifles as they did platoon attacks over Cathcart Castle Golf Course or engaged in fierce house to house fighting down Roddinghead Road. Occasionally one had the honour to act as platoon runner, although the messages issued to us were destined for homes rather than headquarters and usually contained domestic instructions rather than military intelligence. . . . .

Roddinghead Road

Other signs of war became manifest to us. As petrol became unobtainable, so boys no longer came to school by car, but came on foot or bicycles, or by Western S.M.T. bus now painted overall in wartime grey. Street names were obliterated and signposts removed, causing far more confusion to local travellers than to any German parachutists or spies who might happen to be in the district. There was very little traffic on the road except military transport.

In the neighbourhood Rouken Glen was closed off except for the immediate vicinity of the pond and the park was designated a military area. The barbed wire and the sentries convinced us that it was the headquarters of a highly secret and vital military operation but we learned much later that it was nothing more important than a vast parking lot for unwanted RASC 3-tonners . . . . On one occasion we counted 60 army lorries in convoy before we could cross over the road.

A Decontamination Centre was built in the field opposite where the Broom Church now stands and another in a field just south of Mearns Cross. With their sinister implications of gas chambers and poison gas these were given a wide berth by schoolboys fearful of catching some terrifying disease . . . . .

The King and Queen paid a visit to Clydebank to see the bombed areas and the shipyards. They came up by Royal train which was parked in a siding at Whitecraigs Station. Some of us went down to have a look at it, but it appeared to be a very ordinary train with sleeper coaches painted a camouflaged grey colour. It did however reassure us that the Government must have thought that the south side of Glasgow was a safe place to live.

National Geographic maps were put up on classroom walls and we followed the progress of the Allied Armies with red arrows on the maps.

Belmont House School under its present headmaster, Mr John Mercer, continues to flourish and since 1977 has offered boys an all-through education to the Higher Grade of the Scottish Certificate of Education Examinations. Most pupils now entering Belmont do so with the intention of staying until the age of 17–18. This lively community centred on one of Mearns's few Victorian mansions can certainly look to the next century with confidence.

Belmont House

Balgray House

Over the hill from Belmont, and lying east of the Church of Broom and Kirkhill Primary School, is KIRKHILL HOUSE: a family home until the early sixties. It then became the Thomson Television College. Residential courses on broadcasting and film-making were attended by students from many parts of the world until the College closed in the mid-eighties. Kirkhill House is now the Headquarters of Cameron Communications, a company trading in the field of Interactive Video. It supplies IBM with special interactive touch screen training systems utilising the Philips Laserdisc player and promotes the sale of Domesday in Scotland.

Three Georgian mansion houses survive: BALGRAY, CAPELRIG and GREENBANK. Only Balgray, the smallest, remains as a family home; Capelrig House belongs to Eastwood District Council; Greenbank to the National Trust for Scotland. In 'The Old Country Houses of the Old Glasgow Gentry', published in the 1870s, both Capelrig and Greenbank feature.

Greenbank estate dates from the 1760s when Glasgow merchant Robert F. Allason had the house built in policies extending to 15½ acres. It has had many owners, the last of whom, Mr and Mrs William Blyth, presented the property to the National Trust in 1976. A Gardening Advice Centre has been established. Every February the woodlands are carpeted with single and double snowdrops and later in the spring many varieties of narcissus and rhododendron bloom. Within the walled garden, shrubs, flowers, fruit and vegetables are cultivated, demonstrating clearly which plants best tolerate West of Scotland climatic conditions at 500 feet above sea level. Where the tennis court used to lie are glass houses and a garden which provides opportunities for disabled visitors to try out various gardening aids. The ruins of an old sun-dial stand in the centre of the garden. At any time of the year it is a pleasure to walk in the garden and grounds. In summer, demonstrations are arranged and the "Friends of Greenbank" run a small shop selling plants, refreshments and National Trust goods.

Six years after Greenbank House was built, another fine country house for the 'Glasgow gentry' was built at Capelrig. Two hundred years later when the estate was chosen as the site for the new Eastwood School, Capelrig House was threatened with demolition. Under the title:

Birney Boyd, an American pupil, offered the readers of the 1969 Eastwood Magazine the fruits of his researches into the Capelrig site.

𝔜e 𝔒lde 𝔖chool ....?
or
𝔎irks, cart—horses, knights & crosses

Faced with Eastwood's sleek, gleaming exterior of plate glass and concrete, it is easy to forget (if one knew it to begin with) that behind the school's modern facade lurks a bottomless abyss of history and legend to entrap the unwary pupil who begins by wondering . . . .

Here then is what one such unwary pupil, forgetting that curiosity killed the cat, managed to dredge up from the abyss before coming up for air.

The school badge, adopted in 1965, provides an illustrated summary of the school's history. But it is not merely a 'badge' — it is a complete coat of arms, the granting of which entailed a lengthy and detailed correspondence with Lord Lyon King of Arms, several alterations from the original design in accordance with the laws and traditions of heraldry, and not least the payment of a £52 fee to the Government.

The trees, symbolising Eastwood, the parish in which the school was founded in 1937, have been an integral part of the succession of badges. When in 1965 the school moved to its new premises at Capelrig, an area rich in historical lore, several new (or rather old) chapters were added to the history connected with the school.

157

The name 'Capelrig' which occurs in a 12th century document, is thought to be derived from 'Chapel-Ridge', suggesting that there may at one time have been a church situated on the estate. In 1300, Herbert de-Maxwell endowed a chapel in Mearns, perhaps at Capelrig, but today there remains no evidence of this; although in 1927, an archaeologist A.D. Lacaille, discovered the "outline of some ancient structure much disguised by a stable partly built over it . . . . possibly the original chapel."

The two crosses on the badge are a reminder that the Knights Templar once owned the lands of Capelrig (the Knights Templar used a single red cross on a white background as their emblem. The colours have been reversed in the Eastwood badge). The Knights Templar were founded in 1119 and introduced into Scotland by David I (1124–1153). They took vows of poverty (riding two on one horse), chastity and obedience, and were established to care for Christian pilgrims visiting the Holy Land, and to defend the Temple and Holy Sepulchre in Jerusalem from the Saracens. They were half-soldiers, half-monks and eventually gained land in every parish in Scotland.

Because by 1320 they could afford a horse each, they were suppressed and their possessions given to the Knights of St John, who must not have had any vows of poverty to violate. One of the pleasant responsibilities they relinquished was the care of the pits and gallows — the gallows for hanging men and the pits for drowning women. ("Hangin's too good fur 'em!")

However, history and legend go back farther than the 12th century. A clump of trees on the brow of a hill at Capelrig goes by the name of "Devil's Plant'ain" (plantation) and was left untouched to the evil spirits in hopes that they would in return leave the farms of the local people unmolested.* There are no records to show whether their efforts at appeasement were successful or not.

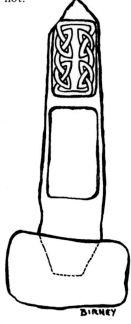

BIRNEY

The Capelrig Cross, an ancient Celtic monument, would have been considered old by the Templars when they first settled on the estate. The oldest relic of Christianity in the parish, it dates from around 900 A.D. and originally stood in a field north-east of Capelrig House. Only the shaft remains, which was removed to

* The road from Mearnskirk to Eaglesham loops round a similar clump of trees to keep the De'il at bay.

Kelvingrove Art Gallery in 1926 but, judging by its proportions, experts reckon it must have ranked as one of the tallest in Renfrewshire. The carvings covering the cross are typical of monuments of its size and date, except for a rather unusual design formed by the arrangement of knots in the top panel on the front of the cross.

There is an ancient legend connected with this cross. Its original site was said to be one of the points of an isosceles triangle, the second point of which was located in the middle of Ryat Linn Reservoir, one and a half miles west-by-south of Capelrig. The secret position of the third point remains a mystery, but he who discovers it and digs in the centre of the triangle shall find a treasure fit to maintain a king. This has never been disproved.

During the Reformation, Sir James Sandelands, Knight of Malta and preceptor of the Order of Hospitallers in Scotland, quickly adopted the reformed religion and in 1563 Queen Mary rewarded his heroic prudence by turning the lands of the order at Capelrig into an Honorary Lordship. Dropping his title Lord St John, he was created Lord Torphichen.

In 1567 the Temple lands of Renfrewshire were acquired by Bryce Semple of Beltrees, from whom Capelrig later passed to the Muirs of Caldwell. After the Restoration in 1660, the land of Covenanters was confiscated. One of their leaders was William Muir, the owner of Capelrig, who fled to Holland. His estates were granted to General Thomas Dalziel of Binns, commander of the Royal forces at Rullian Green, for successfully persecuting the Covenanters.

In a document dated 1670, we find: "Charles R . . . . considering the good and faithful service done to His Majesty and His Majesty's most Royal Father, of ever-blessed Memory . . . . ordains a charter to be passed . . . . granting and disposing to the said Thomas Dalziel . . . . all and Haill the lands of Kippelrig, called of old a Temple-land."

After the Revolution in 1688, Capelrig was restored to the Muir family who retained it until Robert Barclay bought it in 1765. In 1769 he built Capelrig House "a neat handsome house, three stories high, rustic cornered with eleven steps of a stone stair up to the front door." When Robert Barclay died the estate fell to his niece, who married into the Brown family.

The Watch Tower near Patterton Station was known as "Spy House" and was built by George Brown in the late 18th century so that guests at Capelrig could watch the coursing of hounds (hare hunting with dogs). Capelrig House is considered one of the best small Georgian mansions in Scotland and has been given an "A" rating by the Ministry of Works. The two-storey section of the right wing was added in 1913.

During 1959—60 Capelrig was considered and selected as the site for building a new school. When the new Eastwood was completed in 1966, the Education Committee planned to demolish the old house. An article in the *Mercury and Advertiser* announcing this intention was brought to the notice of the Georgian Society by a local resident, resulting in a visit from the Society and a report confirming the architectural merit of the house. The Secretary of State for Scotland also became interested and when it became apparent that planning permission would be granted only if the house was retained, the County Council offered Capelrig House to the District Council.

After £40,000 had been spent by the District Council to arrest almost forty years of neglect, Capelrig House became a community centre. Among the groups using the building are Baptists, originally members of Queen's Park Church, but since 1985 worshipping as a separate congregation under their own minister.

Eastwood School was built as part of Renfrewshire's reorganisation of secondary schooling in Eastwood district in a two-tier system. Younger secondary pupils attended Woodfarm and Williamwood High Schools and older pupils the 'new' Eastwood. This system, which was comprehensive only in S1 and S2 and selective thereafter, was superseded by the present all-through secondary schools in the late 1970s. Nowadays post-primary children in Newton Mearns attend Eastwood or Mearns Castle non-denominational High Schools or travel to St Ninian's Roman Catholic High School in Eastwood Park (formerly Lord Weir's Estate). The science wing of Eastwood School was totally destroyed by fire in 1984, but these laboratories are being rebuilt in time for the Jubilee Celebrations in 1987.

Much then has changed in and around the 'big hooses' of Mearns as the twentieth century has advanced. With the children of school age numbering thousands rather than a few hundred, gone too are the days of the kind of largesse recorded in Mearns School's Log for 22nd June, 1911:—

> To honour the Coronation of King George V. and Queen Mary, all Mearns school children received a medal from Mrs Marshall of Crookfur and a silver sixpence from the Misses Anderson of Hazeldean.
>
> After the medals were presented, led by a piper, the children marched through the village, first to a "cinematographic exhibition" in the new Church Hall and then to games and races in Gilmour's fields. Each child was given a pie and milk and proceedings closed with all singing the National Anthem.

NEW FACES . . . . . .
and NEW PLACES

Like all Scottish places with any aspirations to a 'history' Mearns
has its castle. A real, old keep!

Miscellaneous Observations – 1796 – The only antiquity
here is the Castle of Mearns. It is a large square tower, situated
on a rocky eminence and commanding an extensive and beautiful
prospect. It is not known when it was built. It is supposed to be
several hundred years old and to have been used as a place of
defence. It was surrounded by a strong wall and the entrance
was secured by a draw-bridge. It is now, however, greatly dis-
mantled and out of repair, the family of Blackhall, to whom it
belongs, having their residence at Ardgowan.*

1832 – An ancient square tower is still pointed out, which
passes under the name of the Old Castle of Mearns. This was
formerly the chief seat of the Maxwells. It has lately been roofed
in and is surmounted with a flagstaff. The roof is so contrived
that, being invisible from without, it does not disfigure the
building. On a late occasion, the ancient echoes of the antique
warlike fortalice were awaked after a sleep of centuries to the
voice of music and the nimble cadence of the 'light fantastic
toe.'*

No longer is the castle "out of repair" and it may well again
echo "to the voice of music" as, since 1972, it has been incorporated into Maxwell Mearns Parish Church of Scotland.

Maxwell Mearns Church carried the name MAXWELL from its
former parish in the Kingston district of Glasgow where it had
closed in the sixties after a ministry of over a hundred years.
Coincidentally, MAXWELL is the first recorded name in the
history of Mearns Castle. On 15th March 1449 King James II
granted Herbert, first Lord Maxwell of Caerlaverock and Mearns,
a licence

* 1st and 2nd Statistical Accounts.

164

to big a castle or fortalice on the Baronie of Mearns, to surround
it with strong walls and ditches, to strengthen it with iron gates,
and to erect on top of it all warlike apparatus necessary for its
defence.

These were indeed turbulent times. The south, west, and north
walls are 8 feet thick; and the east 10 feet as the position was
more vulnerable from attack from that direction. The landfall
to the N.W. and S. offered natural defence and the east was
further protected by a ditch spanned by a draw-bridge. The castle
is 45 feet high with three floors. No evidence exists of its ever
having been taken.

The main entrance was an arched doorway eleven feet up the
east wall, presumably reached by a moveable wooden staircase
of some sort. An iron-studded door below this at ground level led
into a dungeon-like area, cold enough for salted carcasses to be
stored during winter. The upper floors were heated by log fires.
A minstrels' gallery suggests festivities — perhaps when, as legend
has it, Mary Queen of Scots and Henry, Lord Darnley, visited the
castle prior to the Battle of Langside. On old maps the hillock to
the east of the castle is called King Harry's Knowe.

Later, conventicles occasionally took place in the castle but
that ceased when it was occupied by dragoons, who were
garrisoned there to patrol the Mearns, Eaglesham and Fenwick
Moors and disperse Covenanting worshippers who might gather
there. The castle changed ownership several times and was
gradually neglected — as reported in the early Statistical Accounts.

How pleasant it is for the castle to live again; and with a
peaceful and welcoming aspect instead of the daunting facade of a
fortress. Estate agents even give it a positive rating in their house
advertisements, for example: the "light, airy lounges" of Broom
Cliff luxury flats "have French windows to sunny balconies
and most flats have views to historic Mearns Castle standing on
its tree-covered knoll."

Church or ruin, the castle has always been a local vantage point.
When Caleb of the *Citizen* met the poet Robert Pollok's brother
David at Waterfoot to be escorted up the valley of the Earn to
the Pollok family home at Moorhouse, they made a detour to
survey the countryside from the top of the castle. Judging from

the eloquence of his description, Caleb found their detour worth-while:

> We now ascend to the battlements of the tower from which we obtain a splendid prospect of the surrounding country. In the south are the dreary moors of Eaglesham, swelling upward to Ballygeich, and fretted with numerous flocks and herds. Westward, amidst a very sea of verdant knolls, clumps of woods and yellow fields, are Mearns Kirk and the Newton, with Dod Hill and Neilston Pad in the distance. To the north and east is the great valley of the Clyde, studded with towns, villages, and mansions, while the Renfrewshire, Kilpatrick, and Campsie Hills rise proudly beyond and the blue mountains of the Gael are faintly visible on the misty horizon.
>
> Beautiful indeed is the wavy bosom of the Mearns, as it lies outspread before us in the warm sunshine of the autumn noon. Merry groups are busy in the fields and the blue smoke curling over cottage and hall gives pleasant indication of happy hearths.

A hundred years and more on, Mearns Kirk and the hills still form part of the distant view, but "merry groups" nowadays in the foreground will comprise young people and adults en route to and from classes and activities in Mearns Castle High School and Community Centre, next 'door' to Maxwell Mearns Church — lots of new faces around a very old place.

166

The change in character of Mearns dates from the 1930s when 1600 new houses were built, 300 by Renfrew County Council south-west of the village and 1300 privately south-east and east. Further changes were arrested, of course, when all building ceased throughout World War II and its aftermath. Before the War the population had doubled from the 1931 census figure of 4,635 and remained under 10,000 until house-building resumed in the late 1950s. The main private builders were Mactaggart and Mickel in Broom Estate and east of Mearns Road; and John Lawrence between Ayr Road and Stewarton Road. The present population is about 20,000. Almost the only open land remaining between Mearns and the adjacent suburbs of Thornliebank, Giffnock, and Clarkston, is the 'green belt' formed by Rouken Glen Park, Whitecraigs Golf Course and Cathcart Castle Golf Course.

Golf courses account for much of 'green' Mearns: three to the north, the two already mentioned and a third within Rouken Glen Park at Deaconsbank: and three to the south, East Renfrewshire, Eastwood and Bonnyton. The Eastwood Club moved from Giffnock to its present moorland course between the Wars when

LOCH AND GOLF COURSE, NEWTON MEARNS

houses were built at Orchard Park. After the Second World War, when many clubs did not admit Jewish members, the Jewish community bought the public course on Bonnyton Moor and founded their own club (which exercises no such exclusions). Many conifers were planted, giving some shelter to the fairways and enhancing the bare moorland without obscuring the spectacular views – west and south to the Firth of Clyde and Arran; north across the city to the Campsie Fells, Kilpatrick Hills and Ben Lomond beyond.

Most Jewish families in Glasgow have lived south of the River Clyde, at first in Gorbals, then gradually moving southwards into Shawlands, Langside, Giffnock, Clarkston and Newton Mearns. The Star of David landmark on Ayr Road, opposite Mearns School, identifies one of Mearns's two synagogues, that of the New Glasgow Congregation. The modern building behind it (entered from Larchfield Avenue) is one of Glasgow's seven orthodox synagogues. 1879 saw the opening of the first synagogue in Scotland – at Garnethill – a gathering-place for the 700 Jews who then lived in Glasgow. They were mostly merchants and businessmen of German and Dutch origin. From the turn of this century, however, to escape growing restrictions in Tsarist Russia and its empire in the Ukraine, Lithuania, Latvia and Poland, thousands of Jewish refugees moved westwards seeking freedom to carry on their businesses, educate their children, and practise their religion. By 1930 four million Jews had left Eastern Europe, the majority of whom travelled to the Americas and to Palestine. About a quarter of a million, however, chose to settle in the United Kingdom and in 1935 Glasgow's Jewish population was estimated at 15,000. Emigration to Israel has since reduced this total, but of the remaining 10,000, many are among the 'new faces' of Newton Mearns.

The expanding population of Newton Mearns is served by an ever increasing range of institutions, one of the most frequented being the District Council Library in its attractive modern building at the end of the Shopping Centre Mall. The Library has all the facilities one would expect, including the opportunity to read agendas and minutes of the monthly meetings of Mearns Community Council. Established in 1977 "to ascertain, to co-ordinate and to express to the Local Authorities the view of the local community" this Council is an 'official' voice for Mearns. Two of its services are the organisation of the bottle-bank and the Mearns Mini-Marathon, which attracts hundreds of participants each May.

The Library occupies ground which, with the Trustee Savings Bank Building, was once an excellent ironmongery business which, as the following advertisement shows, proudly owned Newton Mearns's first telephone number.

Telephone No. 1 Newton Mearns

ROBERT JOHNSTON & SONS

Joiners, Cartwrights,
Blacksmiths, Ironmongers

KILMARNOCK ROAD, NEWTON MEARNS

_ _ _ _ _ _ _ _ _ _ _ _

Carts, Lorries and all kinds of Vehicles
BUILT TO ORDER

All kinds of Jobbing & Blacksmith Work
CAREFULLY EXECUTED

Estimates given for all classes of Joiner Work, etc.

Always in Stock:
FENCING STOBS, RAILS, BARBED WIRE, PLAIN WIRE,
NETTING WIRE, STAPLES

Large Stock of Ironmongery always on hand.
All Household Utensils

_ _ _ _ _ _ _ _ _ _ _ _

EVERYTHING THE FARMER REQUIRES

LUBRICATING AND BURNING OILS SUPPLIED

By the 1930s the telephone numbers were approaching three thousand and a new exchange was required. This 1936 Telephone Exchange Building (in Ayr Road between Firwood Road and Knowes Road) carries an insignia rare in Britain — the royal crest of King Edward VIII. Between the Library and the Telephone Exchange at 202 Ayr Road, is a Greek Thomson villa — Croyland (formerly Rysland).

170

Kilmarnock Road, Newton Mearns

MEARNS ROAD, NEWTON MEARNS

The considerable increase in population in the second half of this century is not the result of the coming of new industry. Mearns has become almost entirely residential: to live and to work in Newton Mearns nowadays is the exception rather than the rule, a reversal of life-style from earlier days. Only one manufacturing enterprise of any size is operational. After a gap of six years, English Sewing Ltd. re-opened the Netherplace Works in 1986 for thread dyeing and runs them in conjunction with their Neilston factory. Its metal-faced chimney, and the brick stack of Mearnskirk Hospital, are the only two conspicuous chimney landmarks in the Mearns area. A century ago bleaching, printing and dyeing works operated at Hazeldean, Broom and the Tofts, all the works being located to benefit from the damp air and abundant supply of soft water. Early in the century the Tofts

Company built larger works at Netherplace and by the thirties the only reminder of their original location was the manager's house – Tofts House. It survives still, surrounded by trees and the many houses of Rodger and Lambie Avenues. The fortunes of this Netherplace cloth finishing firm – Wallace & Company, then Tootal – have fluctuated considerably; and from 1980 to 1986 the works were closed after running down for several years. It's

Netherplace Bleach Works Mearns

hard to believe now that at one time there were rows of workers' cottages at both Netherplace and Tofts. The cottages at Tofts were across from and behind "Greenside" in the valley below St Cadoc's Primary School.

This Roman Catholic school takes its name from St Cadoc's Church – in Barrhead Road from 1966 until 1981 – now in Fruin Avenue on a picturesque site backed by the woods behind Rysland and Forestfield Avenues and overlooking Whitecraigs Golf Course. The name CADOC honours an ancient British saint of the 6th century. Associated mainly with monastic foundations in Wales, Cadoc also lived for some years on the island of Rhuys off Brittany. He visited Jerusalem, Rome, Cornwall and Strathclyde (then an ancient British kingdom: capital Dumbarton). It is possible that his visit was at the invitation of Kentigern (Mungo), the first bishop of the Strathclyde Britons, who had spent some years in exile in Wales in Cadoc's lifetime. Cadoc is said to have died a martyr's death in the struggles of the Britons against the conquering Saxons. Other forms of the name are DOCUS, CATHMAEL and CADVAEL.

This choice of a British saint from the old Celtic form of Christianity for a church and school in Mearns fits well with theories about the origin of the name MEARNS itself. The Rev. MacKellar opened his Second Statistical Account by citing six forms of the word — MEARNS MEARNIS MERNES MEIRNES MORNESS MAERONAS — and elaborating thus:

> The name of this Parish first appears in authentic form in the Chartulary of Glasgow, and in Prynne, as far back as the year 1296 — the eventful period when Edward I of England made his celebrated attempt to wrest from the hands of Scotsmen their rights and privileges and to annex Scotland's ancient crown and sceptre permanently to the throne of England. The power of Edward's arms was felt and acknowledged throughout the better portion of the Lowlands of Scotland, and many a wealthy ecclesiastic and proud noble were constrained to bow the neck and swear fealty to the common enemy. Among the many victims to the power of England, John Petit of the MEIRNES is mentioned in the records of the times as one of the barons of the day who swore fealty to Edward I.

> The spelling of the name of this parish, like all other ancient names, varies exceedingly . . . . the oldest form is MEIRNES, as above, but it is also frequently styled MERNES, MEARNIS, MEIRNES, and MORNESS.

> O'Brien in his Word-Book derives the modern name MEARNS from the British MAERONAS — a name exactly descriptive of this parish: "a district inhabited by herdsmen.' . . . . this parish has ever been distinguished as a district for pasturage and at the present day the produce of the dairy . . . . obtains a ready and favourite market in the neighbouring city of Glasgow. A continuation of the same sort of pasturage runs into Stewarton and Dunlop, which last place gives its name to the best sort of cheese manufactured in the West of Scotland.

Perhaps originally the name was not applied to any *particular* place but was a general appellation applicable to an indefinite extent of pastoral country. This in later times took the names of the Kirk Towns, or more conspicuous villages with which the several places composing it were respectively connected. That somewhat extensive district lying between the rivers Dee and North Esk . . . . is still occasionally known by the appellation of 'the Mearns'.

A view similar to O'Brien's is offered by Boyd Scott in *Old Days and Ways in Newton Mearns.* He associates the name with the ancient British princes of Strathclyde, among whose land officers one rank was designated MAER . . . . steward of a MAERONI . . . . later anglified as MEARNS.

Whatever significance may attach to the word MEARNS one thing is certain – the word *NEWTON* has long lost any literal meaning. Newton Mearns, new as much of it is, has a very long history. The identity of the area is, however, swiftly changing as more and more houses are built and more and more families settle. I visited Primary 7 pupils in Mearns School, about a quarter of whom have lived in the area for less than two years, and invited them to speculate about Mearns at the end of the 20th century.

Responses were predictably diverse and ranged from the mundane to the exotic, the gloomy to the bold:

- it will stay more or less the same
- there will be lots more houses and shops
- where I live is near green fields — they will probably become housing estates
- Mearns will have changed a lot
- busier because the motorway will be finished
- it will be bigger and more built up and more modern
- the Mearns will be full of film stars
- it will be technological and weird — something that we can't think about just now
- Newton Mearns will be very easy for a person to work in because of computers
- there will be twice as many sports shops around for most people are interested in sport
- there will be no farms
- Newton Mearns will just become part of Glasgow
- there will be more vandals and things like that
- it will be different because of more houses and important buildings — more parks and facilities
- Mearns will become a City
- it might expand and could be the centre of Glasgow

Who can say? How pleasant nonetheless to imagine burgh status for Newton Mearns — with the Cross as town centre, quieter presumably as the M77 bypass will have diverted much of the traffic. Flower gardens stretch from the War Memorial round the Shopping Centre to Robshill and the park . . . trees and shrubs shade the car parks and soften the gaunt exteriors of the Centre, the new Post Office, the hotel and leisure centre . . . seats abound . . . fountains play . . .

Such an environment would offer the young Crookfur poets themes to celebrate rather than lament. The quality of their writing, and the obvious sensitivity of the writers, engenders optimism about the future of Newton Mearns. Let's conclude with another poem from their prize-winning collection:

How old were you, Oak Tree, when they cut you down,
And how many seasons had you seen?
How many winters were you white with snow,
And how many summers were you green?

How old were you, Oak Tree, when they cut you down,
And how many creatures had you fed?
How many people smiled to see you there,
And how many wept when you were dead?

How much shelter and how much food
And acorns buried by the dyke?
And how many wasps came buzzing round your trunk
To find a cosy lining for their byke?

No more corncrake and no more owl,
No children playing round your feet.
Couldn't they have left you for a few more years
Standing at the corner of the street?

178

BOOKS AND BOOKLETS
consulted follow in chronological order of their publication:—

1775	John Howie: *The Scots Worthies*
1791–98	*First Statistical Account*
1823	Robert Pollok: *Tales of the Covenanters*
1827	Robert Pollok: *The Course of Time*
1834–45	*Second Statistical Account*
1842	*Recreations of Christopher North*
1846	David Pollok: *Life of Robert Pollok*
1854	Caleb: *Rambles Round Glasgow*
1919	Mearns Cattle Show Programme
1920	T.C.F. Brotchie: *Tramways Guide*
1939	A. Boyd Scott: *Old Days and Ways in Newton Mearns*
1939	J.A. Strang: *A History of Mearns Parish* (3 volumes, bound typescript)
1941	*Hansard*, Volumes 371 and 372
1944–62	*Third Statistical Account*
1949	Mearnskirk and Peter Pan: Souvenir Brochure
1950	Churchill: *The Second World War*
1955	Mearnskirk Hospital 1930–1955: Pictorial Album
1964	Eden: *Memoirs: The Reckoning*
1969	Year Book of Mearns Horticultural Society
1969	Eastwood School Magazine
1970	Henry Hay: *Newton Mearns Past and Present*
1971	James Douglas-Hamilton: *Motive for a Mission*
1976	Royal Observer Corps: *Hess Affair; May 10, 1941*
1976	Mearns School Centenary Magazine
1979	Belmont House School Golden Jubilee Magazine
1980	Mearnskirk Hospital Golden Jubilee Pictorial Album
1982	*Twelve Centuries of Christian Witness at Mearns Parish Church*
1984	C. Hutt and H. Kaplan: *A Scottish Shtetl*
1986	M. Glickman: *The Glasgow Jewish Community*

WARMEST THANKS

to   *Miss Rae Mackinlay, Mrs J.S. Osborne, Miss E. Menzies, Mrs E.C. Dobson, Miss Bowman, Thomas L. Craig, Dr and Mrs Fordyce, Mrs Ella Cormack, Mrs Annie Lewis, Mrs Mary Dinsmor, David Arthur, James Anderson, John Anderson, Mrs Maisie Anderson, Miss I.H. Russell, A.M.R. Russell, James* and *Marianne Deas, R.S. Barclay, Miss E.A. Calder,* and *the Rev. W. Murray Mackay*
for sharing their recollections of earlier Mearns in conversation;

to   *Miss Marion S. McFarlane* and *Alasdair Morrison* on whose efforts ⟨4⟩ largely depends; *Lord James Douglas-Hamilton* for permission to quote from his book on Hess; *Sheriff Neil S. Gow* for much of ⟨7⟩ ; *Michael Moss,* Glasgow University Archivist, for advice and access to the Scottish Business Archive; *Janice Howie,* formerly of the Eastwood District Library Local History Project, for access to her material; *Mrs Marion Howie* for permission to include poems by her pupils; *the Greater Glasgow Health Board* for text and photographs about Mearnskirk Hospital; *the Glasgow Room* of the Mitchell Library and *Outram Press* for material from *The Bulletin* and other newspapers;

and for photographs to *A.M.R. Russell, Mary Dinsmor, David Arthur, Walter Clark, Mrs J.S. Osborne, Ailsa King, Anne Robertson, David Kidd, K.A.C. Melvin* and *Peter Cowley.*

"Men in their generation are like the leaves in the trees. The wind blows and one year's leaves are scattered on the ground; but the trees burst into bud and put on fresh ones when spring comes round."

(Homer)